HAPPY CHAOS

HAPPY CHAOS

Soleil Moon Frye

· · · · · · · · · · · · · · · ·

From Punky to Parenting *and*
My Perfectly Imperfect Adventures In Between

DUTTON

DUTTON
Published by Penguin Group (USA) Inc.
375 Hudson Street, New York, New York 10014, U.S.A.
Penguin Group (Canada), 90 Eglinton Avenue East, Suite 700, Toronto, Ontario M4P 2Y3,
Canada (a division of Pearson Penguin Canada Inc.); Penguin Books Ltd, 80 Strand, London
WC2R 0RL, England; Penguin Ireland, 25 St Stephen's Green, Dublin 2, Ireland (a division
of Penguin Books Ltd); Penguin Group (Australia), 250 Camberwell Road, Camberwell,
Victoria 3124, Australia (a division of Pearson Australia Group Pty Ltd); Penguin Books
India Pvt Ltd, 11 Community Centre, Panchsheel Park, New Delhi—110 017, India; Penguin
Group (NZ), 67 Apollo Drive, Rosedale, Auckland 0632, New Zealand (a division of Pearson
New Zealand Ltd); Penguin Books (South Africa) (Pty) Ltd, 24 Sturdee Avenue, Rosebank,
Johannesburg 2196, South Africa

Penguin Books Ltd, Registered Offices: 80 Strand, London WC2R 0RL, England

Published by Dutton, a member of Penguin Group (USA) Inc.

First printing, August 2011
10 9 8 7 6 5 4 3 2 1

REGISTERED TRADEMARK—MARCA REGISTRADA

LIBRARY OF CONGRESS CATALOGING-IN-PUBLICATION DATA
has been applied for.

ISBN 978-0-525-95231-2

Printed in the United States of America
Set in Bell MT
Designed by Spring Hoteling

This book is dedicated to my two children, who fill my life with so much love and Happy Chaos each and every day, and to my nieces, whose laughter and smiling faces bring so much joy to us.

To my big bro and his wife, who have shown us to live every day as a new adventure. To my mother, who taught me to never stop believing in myself or the world around us. To Mema, Bapu, and my dad. I love you now and always. To everyone who taught me that sometimes the best lessons come when we fall down and get back up again, and to my husband, who I fell in love with from the moment we first met. I love you more today than ever before and like we said when it all began: "As my sweet dreams of childhood come true, I am so grateful to dream them with you."

Contents

Contents

Contents

HAPPY CHAOS

1

Welcome to Happy Chaos

Question of the day: If you were going to write a book about the story of your life, what would the title be?

"Short Girls Have Feelings, Too."

—Dana

"It would probably be *No Regrets*. I have no regrets in life, just learning experiences! Life is too short to regret."

—Tracey

"The heart of a mother: My journey to mommyhood through open adoption."

—Stephanie

"I think it would have to be called *The Trails*. I've noticed that no matter how you cut it, no one goal in life has a direct route. So you keep following different lines till you get there."

—Gary

was seven years old when I walked onto the set of *Punky Brewster*, a show about a little girl who was abandoned by her mother in a grocery store. I think of it now and smile as I imagine them pitching the series. A show about a kid whose parents abandoned her at the tender age of seven . . . and it's a comedy! Then she narrowly escapes being sent to an orphanage . . . an orphanage! This wasn't a drama—or a novel by Dickens—this was a prime-time sitcom on NBC. Amazing. Even more amazing, Punky wasn't saved from the orphanage by a mom and a dad with a big house and a backyard. Instead, she and her dog, Brandon, were taken in by a grumpy old man. And together they made a family.

Punky became a champion for all nontraditional families, and I spent some of the happiest, most incredible, adventurous, hilarious years of my life playing that little girl. I like to think that there's still a lot of Punky in me. Or maybe there was a lot of me in Punky. In many ways, I'm still that same inquisitive, boundary-questioning kid that I played on television.

Throughout my whole life, as soon as I could talk, I was asking why. Not just the usual *why is the sky blue?* kind of questions. No, I wanted to know how the world worked. I was fascinated by human behavior. I vividly remember that as early as preschool, I was already wondering how I got here. I just had to know where babies came from, and I wasn't satisfied with vague answers. I wanted detail. So my free-spirited mom gave me *Where Do Babies Come From?* This book offered the complete lowdown—including diagrams of the male and female anatomy. Little did she know, I tucked that wonderfully informative little book into my school bag, and the next day I played show-and-tell with my wide-eyed classmates.

There was some drama with the other parents at the school after that, but you know, knowledge is meant to be shared! The really remarkable thing about all of my questioning is that I didn't even speak my first words until I was three years old. And of course my first sentence was a question: "Mommy, how do you like my painting?"

Then I grew up (sort of), and eventually I became a mom myself, and I had *so* many questions. Again, I looked at books, but most of them didn't really seem to speak to me. And then I looked at the other parents around me—the ones who seemed to have this parenting thing down really well—and I wondered if maybe there was a secret manual they all read, and somehow I didn't get my copy. It felt like other moms opened their strollers with a neat flick of the wrist while blue-birds sang around their heads. Meanwhile, I'd still be struggling to get mine open, and wondering, "What's that smell?" before discovering that I'd managed to walk out of the house with baby vomit in my hair.

In my search for answers I read books, blogs, and magazine articles, and everything just seemed so . . . perfect. I'd see a blog where the mom was cutting vegetables on the counter, and the baby was sitting quietly (and cleanly) beside her. Okay, I don't know about you, but that is not my life. If I'm cooking pancakes for breakfast, the kids are throwing batter and they have syrup up their arms and strawberry stains on their clothes, my clothes, the furniture. . . . We live a messy, chaotic life. And I love it. But still, every once in a while I wonder—are we crazier than everyone else, or does it just seem like that?

So I dug a little deeper online. And I found some places where people like me were asking their own honest questions.

I discovered the incredible world of social media. I found myself turning to Twitter and Facebook so that I could connect to people like me, the other parents who were leaving the house with clothes on inside out and syrup all over. And then the world opened up. Suddenly here were all of these moms and dads connecting in a way that felt so authentic and genuine. Here was a space where parents could be themselves and speak openly. I found that the more I shared, the more other parents were sharing their stories, and I learned that I wasn't alone as a new parent. There were a lot more parents like me out there, parents who didn't get the secret manual, either. And it was such a relief! Finally, I could take a breath and let it out slowly. It's all right not to be an expert at opening up the stroller or figuring out the car seat—just as long as someone gets the car seat installed properly. It's okay that I still have no idea how to get those plastic toys out of their packaging. All of those little things that for so long had been piling up and making me feel like I came from another planet— suddenly that weight lifted and I realized that there are a *million* other parents who have felt this way. I'm not the only one who's walked into the room to discover her two-year-old drawing on the white walls with a black Sharpie.

It's so easy for us to be hard on ourselves. We compare ourselves to other parents and hold ourselves up to some standard of perfection that we've seen or read about in books—or invented in our own heads. Because of course we want to be perfect for our kids. God knows, if I could, I would! But the vomit in the hair, the pancake batter on the chair, and the black Sharpie on the walls—this is real life. And it's dealing with all that messiness that makes us great parents, and makes us laugh, and makes us stronger.

Instead of being so focused on trying to be perfect, I decided to live my life trying to be the best parent I can be. I like to call myself a work in progress, and I feel like every day I grow as a parent, and I learn something new. There are plenty of books out there that tell you how to do everything perfectly. But those didn't help me when I was feeling really lost and confused. What helped me was knowing that other parents felt the same way that I did.

That's why it was so important to me to write this book. By sharing our messy experiences with each other, we learn that we're not alone. You will see many of my questions throughout the book, along with answers from parents just like us. We will share our proud parenting moments along with our most embarrassing ones, and I will tell you the secrets that no one told me about. If there's any way that I'm an expert, it's this: I know what I know—and I know how much I don't know. So consider this the "Messy Guide to Parenting"—it's the secret manual that I wish I had when I first started out on this incredible parenting journey. Along the way, I'm going to share a few incredibly helpful tips that I've picked up, either from my own experiences or from the amazing wisdom of others. At the end of each chapter, you will see "S.P.S." It stands for Soleil's P.S.—because, yes, I still use P.S. all the time. I can't help it. I'm an eighties girl at heart.

Welcome to *Happy Chaos*. Welcome to the worry, the uncertainty, and the joy. Look at your kid and remember the kid you once were, and get down on the floor and be that kid again. That kid never went away—she's still right in there. And if the laundry is piling up, and your daughter just sprayed the kitchen with a gallon of rainbow sprinkles, and you wonder what that smell is (my advice: check your hair), rest assured that if you opened the door to my house right now, you would find the exact same thing. Sometimes we even go to bed without bathing. With chlorine in our hair. Don't look at me that way. I know! Just don't tell anybody, okay?

Virgil Frye

Here I am as a kid living in "Happy Chaos"

2

. . . .

Let's Have a Baby!

Question of the day: What is your recommended playlist for the labor/delivery room?

"Some relaxing meditation music (for the time I spend not in labor), and a mix from The Beatles to NOFX for when all the 'action' is taking place."

—AnnaMae

"Labor is a different creature altogether. You want some loud music to drown out the contractions, some soothing tunes for those quiet lulls and some high-energy songs to inspire you through to the finish. Authentic South African mixes are great for the delivery room. You just have to look past the fact that the baby will be born to *The Lion King.*"

—Ashley

* "Baby Love"—The Supremes
* "Sweet Child O' Mine"—Guns N' Roses
* "Push It"—Salt-N-Pepa

HAPPY CHAOS

* "This Woman's Work"—Kate Bush
* "I'm Coming Out"—Diana Ross
* "Ordinary Miracle"—Sarah McLachlan

—Jason A. L.

"Something calming. Let's face it when you are in full labour you won't notice music anyway but calming is better than punk!"

—@vanity ace fake:

Bob Marley was playing on the stereo, soft lights decorated the room, friends and family were laughing and swapping stories . . . it was a party—the best party *ever*. And there I was, in the center of it all, pushing out my baby.

That's how we do things in my family. Sure, you can have a baby without the help of everyone you love, but where's the fun in that? When my free-spirited mother was a month overdue with me, my godmother took her out to the local dance hall, where her water broke on the dance floor. Then Mom planned to have me at my godparents' house in Topanga Canyon, but there were complications, and instead of having the perfect earthy at-home birth, my mother found herself on an adventure in the back of the family van. Mom and my godparents tore off through the hills, looking for a hospital that would take her. While my mother labored away on a makeshift bed in the back, hospital after hospital turned them away because she wasn't preregistered. Finally, after driving all the way to Glendora, California, hours away, my godfather found a hospital that accepted my mom. And there I was born, welcomed by all who loved me most in the world.

I hoped for the same kind of experience for my own baby

girl. I daydreamed about what colorful place my water would break. I would be standing in the middle of a party, decked out in all my nine months of glory, and get excited at the idea that a gush of water would appear at any moment. I must have woken my husband up a thousand times during my pregnancy, thinking that I was about to give birth. I was just so excited. I wanted my new baby's first breath of air to be filled with love. I wanted happiness to wrap around her like a force field of strength and protection that would last a lifetime. I found a great doctor who made me feel incredibly comfortable (and who was the crush of every pregnant woman in Hollywood), and in the weeks leading up to Poet's due date, I stayed up late every night making playlists so that her arrival would have the perfect soundtrack. I bought small lights to put around the hospital room, and I packed the softest sheets, a robe, and a pillow from home. I was determined to make the hospital feel like a cross between a spa and a hotel room.

Then, two weeks before Poet was due, my doctor discovered that there wasn't enough amniotic fluid to support her any longer, and we would have to induce. "Today," he said. I still remember the feeling that washed over me. I had thought I was ready for this, but was I ready for *this*? Even Jason couldn't quite grasp that Poet wasn't waiting two more weeks to make her entrance. He actually said, "Do I have to cancel my meetings?" The doctor's response was something like "Yeah, guys, I think you'd better clear the day." We had just enough time to race home and grab the bags stuffed with every item I thought I could possibly need or want. And thus began one of the most amazing, unexpected, and perfectly imperfect experiences of my life.

My labor room was like Thanksgiving, Hanukkah, Christmas, and a birthday party rolled into one big celebration, all to the tune of a folk-reggae soundtrack. While I labored, a group of friends and family came to support us and then stayed for the party. I had brought a little Buddha with me to be a calming focal point, and my loved ones generated waves of nurturing love that reverberated around that room. An amazing number of people were there to welcome Poet into the world: my mom, my godmother, Tori (my best friend since we were two years old), Ashton, Demi (who turned out to be the best birthing coach ever; I swear, she must have been a midwife in a previous life), my good friend Heather, and my mother-in-law. Oh, and the doctor, the nurse, my husband. And me.

I was given Pitocin to move things along. Demi soothed me and gave me a leg massage while I happily sucked on Popsicles. I had enough of an epidural to make labor bearable, but not so much that I couldn't push, and when I'd reached eight centimeters, the doctor came in and announced, "Okay, let's have a baby!" Of course, this was the one moment when Jason and Ashton had stepped out to check on a game on the television in the waiting room down the hall. My tribe of women was surrounding me and said lovingly, "This is it. It's time." Jason quickly came running back into the room. Jason was on one side of me, my mother was on my other side, Tori was at one of my legs, and Demi was at the other. My family and friends cheered me on. The doctor had me push, and then, as Poet started to crown, I will never forget reaching down and feeling her head for the first time. I kept pushing with every bit of my heart and soul as her little body emerged. The doctor said, "Now pull your baby out." I put my hands gently under Poet's arms, pulled her out, and put her on top of me. Then, at 2:20 A.M. on August 24, 2005, the room broke into a joyful chorus of "Happy Birthday."

A few hours after that it was just me, Jason, and our baby.

Jason finally fell asleep, and Poet and I listened to music for the rest of the night, while I stared at her in awe. The next day the room refilled with family, extended family, and friends. One of my most precious memories was watching my godfather, Joseph, hold Poet. He had raced through half of Southern California to find a hospital where I could be born, and now here he was holding my firstborn. He was fighting cancer at the time—and would

Jason and me in total awe of our new baby girl, Poet

die within a year and a half—and I was so overwhelmingly grateful that my baby had these precious moments with him.

Elation carried us through the next few days in the hospital. I remember in the delirious hours after Poet was born, I was so ridiculously joyful that I shouted out, "Let's do it again!" I'm sure half the mothers in the maternity wing thought I was crazy, and the other half wanted to know what drugs I was on. But it was just sheer ecstatic delight. This girl we had waited nine months for—this girl I had truly waited my whole life for—was here, finally. And nothing could distract us from the wonder.

* * *

S.P.S.

Whatever works for you . . .

I had a little Buddha as my calming focal point when I gave birth to Poet, but yours could be anything that's meaningful to you. Maybe it's something spiritual, or maybe it's something comforting from home. I had soft lights that looked like candles and my playlist that I had made at home. I really wanted the room to have a warm feel. And I had lots of people around. Not everyone is going to want eight people in the room, but for us it was perfect. The important thing is to have things that make you feel most comfortable and to make a list of what you want and don't want. Be sure to share it with whoever else you plan to have in the labor room with you. Ask your friends how they did it when they gave birth, and decide for yourself what is the right choice for you. Also have a call list ready of who you want to be contacted after the birth. You can always have a friend call on your behalf. It is a nice way of letting people know that your baby has entered the world.

A few things that help . . .

Chances are you won't be able to eat anything once you're laboring away in the hospital. Most likely, you won't be hungry anyway. But I was really, really thirsty, and for me the best thing was Popsicles. Sweet, cold, and refreshing. Just perfect. Demi gave me the most amazing leg massage, which was awesome. When you're having contractions, your whole body tenses up, and all those muscles can get incredibly tight and sore, so if you have someone you feel really comfortable with massaging you, it can be helpful. Most of all, don't be afraid to ask for what you need.

Just one more thing that no one else seems to want to tell you . . .

So there you are, getting ready to have your baby, and you are pushing like crazy. Pushing, pushing, and then right there on the table, you may just go poop. Now, this doesn't happen to everyone, but it does happen to many women, and it is nothing to be embarrassed about. No book or class ever mentioned this to me, and that is why I feel it is my duty to share it with you. It was one of my very close friends who finally filled me in as I stared at her in disbelief. I got myself so worked up about it that I actually did something a little crazy. Yes, I gave myself an enema right *before* I went into labor, something that is *totally* not medically recommended. So, take it from me, your sometimes too-honest friend Soleil: It might happen, and don't worry about it! It is totally normal and *nothing* to be ashamed of. And if you are supporting someone who is giving birth and she goes number two . . . be supportive and, most important, be nice.

If you're not the one having the baby . . .

Let's face it, the one having the baby is the one who's getting all the attention (at least until the baby's born, and then it's the baby's turn). Your job is to help the pregnant mom bring that baby into the world while keeping your relationship intact! So here's my advice: Long before you get to the hospital, make a list of the things that your partner loves and finds comforting. And most important: Listen to her. Is she cold or hot? Are her lips parched? Offer to get her some lip balm, crushed ice, or a Popsicle. Help her keep her hair out of her face, and ask if she would like the lights softened. You know your partner best. Just remember that labor is different from any other experience you've had (especially if this is your first baby), so be prepared to be flexible and supportive, and if she is having a tough birth, don't take it personally if she starts yelling profanities at you!

Granny Panties

Question of the day: What was the one thing that no one told you about having a baby that you had to find out for yourself?

> "I think one of the most important things we figured out is that 'going by the book' doesn't work for everyone. Sometimes you have to find your own path and make decisions based on what's best for your family."
>
> —JoyfulTxGal

> "No one ever told me I would need to put Vaseline on my son for a month following his circumcision or that the skin could reattach! Ouch!! No one ever told me when to first bring my child to a dentist. No one told me that breastfeeding would be the most challenging and rewarding experience proving to myself that if I put my mind to anything and not give up that I could do it (with a little help from fenugreek, phytolacca, and hepar sulphur). Finally no one ever told me that having babies would be the hardest,

scariest, self-sacrificing, yet most amazing thing ever. You will get through it!"

—Erin

"We are on our third child. The first two are girls and the newborn is a boy. Well our first boy, no one EVER told us to put his 'peepee' down when putting on his diaper. For the first week, we could not figure out why he was wetting his crib, onesie, etc . . . What do you know, we pointed it down and no more wet crib :-) A warning label would have saved us a lot of wet bed sheets."

—Leslie

"That I'd love her instantly and forever :-)"

—Becky

Meeno

My family with Poet and me at the hospital right after she was born

As I was lying with my beautiful baby girl after giving birth, I remember a nurse walking in holding these fishnet granny panties. I stared at her in horror. "For me?" I asked innocently. The woman rolled her eyes at me as she continued holding them, and with her other hand held up a gigantic white surgical glove. For those of you who have had vaginal births, you know what I am talking about. For those who haven't, just picture the biggest fishnet panties you have ever seen and an enormous surgical glove filled with ice. That gigantic ice hand goes right onto your Va-JJ and immediately becomes your best friend. The granny panties hold that glove right in place, and as if things couldn't get sexier, the nurse then handed me a spray can. I was totally perplexed until I learned it was to numb the vagina. Yes, to numb my vagina.

There are so many things that no one tells you about having a baby. Oh sure, I read a few things. I talked to my friends. I did my research. But I swear to you, no one ever told me that after I had my baby I would be handed a gigantic pair of fishnet granny panties. And I'm positive no one told me that I'd be given a spray to numb my vagina. And I am absolutely, one hundred percent certain that no one told me that I would be given an enormous white rubber glove—filled with ice—that I would then stick on my vagina.

Little did I know at that moment how essential to my life these three completely bizarre items would become: mesh panties, vagina spray, ice glove. With that tool kit in hand, the maternity nurse sent me on my way, and we were ready to leave the hospital with our new baby girl. As we signed ourselves out, the only thing the hospital wanted to know was if we had a car seat. That's it. Have a car seat? Here's your baby.

Jason wrestled the car seat into submission, and when we got out on the road we had this feeling that the world as we once knew it had changed—and it had. We drove four miles per hour the whole way home, fearful that any bump or movement might upset our new baby. Had people really done this before? We felt like the first. There I sat looking at my husband and our beautiful baby, thinking about life. My Va-JJ spray was wearing off and reality was sinking in.

When we got to our house, I fell into the warm embrace of my mother's loving arms. I caught the scent of her pasta sauce when we walked in the door, and I knew I was home. And our girl, Poet, was home, too. It was heaven . . . and then I realized that—oh my God—we'd forgotten the placenta at the hospital. I'd been determined to bring it home and plant a tree over it—like the true earth mother I aspired to be. No placenta, no tree, so I called my good friend Hillary, who raced back to the hospital to retrieve our placenta. She ran through the halls of the hospital having no idea where one might go to pick up a placenta—preferably the one that had been attached to my baby and not to someone else's. Finally, knowing that I had my heart set on a placenta tree, she said to a nurse, "Just give me one!" To this day I'm not sure we got the right one, but I try not to think too much about that.

My mother's welcome-home feast was just the beginning of the nurturing. I know that some new moms are brought flowers. Some are brought baby clothes. Me, I get food. Because my family loves to eat, and even by the standards of my food-loving family, I really love food. Neighbors knew the way to my heart, and they stuffed our kitchen. The celebration in the hospital turned into an extended holiday, and the house filled with family, extended family, and friends all stopping by to welcome us home and meet Poet.

I'm sure that I was still on a new-baby high during those days. I barely slept, because I couldn't stop holding Poet. When she was awake, I needed to be awake, and when she was asleep, I just wanted to look at her. And oh, that new-baby smell. It was intoxicating. The rhythm of life those first few weeks was simple and all-consuming—change the baby, hold the baby, feed the baby. And feed the baby. And feed the baby. I loved the incredible bonding experience of breastfeeding, but at one point I broke down and called the doctor and said, "Okay, can your nipples actually fall off?" And I was not kidding.

Everything we did was a first: first bath, first walk, first drive in the car. It was like we walked into an alternate universe that looked just like the old one, but all the rules were different and we had to relearn how to live. I remember the first time we tried to go on an adventure with Poet, and we got halfway down the street only to turn around again because it suddenly occurred to us that maybe it was too soon to take her outside. And the diaper bag—what were you supposed to put in there? I had no clue. Even a simple stroll around the neighborhood was a production. It's hilarious to me now when I think about those days when I took forty-five minutes to get ready in the morning. Now it was a miracle if I could take a shower. Even if Poet was quiet, I'd be convinced that I heard her cries echoing, reverberating through the house. Every few seconds I'd have to leap out of the shower to see if she was okay. Once I was clothed—shirt on inside out— it was time to get her changed and dressed (and hope that she wouldn't poop or spit up even before I'd lifted her off the changing table). I remember how scared I'd be that I would hurt her just bending her little arms to fit them into her onesie, and how fragile she seemed to me.

Then the question was what to carry the baby in. I so badly wanted to use a sling. The other moms made it look so easy and nurturing, their babies snuggled close to their chests, wrapped in brightly colored organic fiber. But I found it to be impossible. I tried wrapping it around my waist, my chest, every possible way before finally giving up and just carrying Poet. The stroller should have been easier, too, but that was another thing I struggled with. I'd study the other mothers closely—a flick of the wrist, and it was open. For me it was the opposite. I would pull it, tug it, kick it, and only after twenty minutes figure it out. Then the next time I would have the same problem.

Every day it was a shock to discover all the things I hadn't known before. So I observed all the parents around me, and I soaked up the knowledge. Within a few weeks, right around the time that Jason had to go back to work, I was starting to get the swing of things in my own way. I had figured out a few things that worked for me: power walking all night long when she cried due to her tummy issues and colic, never getting too comfortable in bed because the second I lay down she would wake up, that she was still breathing after I put my cheek next to her for the twentieth time in the night, that I could function on only a few hours of sleep (I think moms have a superhero gene somewhere inside of them), and finally, that pacifiers were not evil. I knew that hippie moms weren't supposed to use pacifiers. And to that I say: This hippie mom uses a pacifier. And this hippie mom learned the value of walking around in granny panties with an ice pack attached to her vagina.

The first days and weeks of new parenthood can be

surreal, exhilarating, and sometimes scary. Just listen to your heart, listen to your baby, and listen to the nurse when she tells you where to put that ice pack. You don't have to have all of the answers, and it's okay to learn as you go.

Jason and me with Poet after her first bath

* * *

S.P.S.

What I packed for the hospital . . .

Sometimes babies come early and sometimes they come late, so it's better to be prepared. I had a bag packed three weeks before my due date with Poet, and it was a good thing. Ziplocs were my friend when packing, and they still are. They made it easier to separate things for me. Most important is to bring things that are cozy. This meant my snuggliest robe, two pairs of socks, and baggy sweats (remember something comfortable and roomy so you have space for the vagina ice—seriously).

Now, I'm not saying that *you* need all this, and your needs may vary depending on how long you will be there, but here's what I found most helpful to pack for the hospital:

1. My softest sheets from home. Call me crazy, but I wanted the room I was in after labor to feel amazing.

2. My own pillow.

3. Two pairs of sweats (with extra room) and a few sweatshirts and T-shirts.

4. Two pairs of cozy socks and several pairs of underwear—granny panties, not G-strings.

5. A soft robe.

6. My own towel (a little over the top, maybe).

7. Soft lights—the ones that look like candles are amazing! This creates a warm feel.

8. My iPod and speaker loaded with my favorite music and a camera to document all the moments. Don't forget the charger!

9. Some of our favorite snacks.

10. A diary and pen to write down the highlights of the experience.

11. A little toiletry bag filled with my favorite products and a toothbrush.

12. For the baby, a swaddle and a few newborn changes along with a baby cap and booties, something that covers their hands and feet. Easy access is key.

About that car seat . . .

Jason and I thought it was hilarious that the only proof of competence that we needed in order to take our baby home from the hospital was that we had a car seat. I mean, of course a car seat is essential, but what if we had no idea what to do with the baby once we got her home? Anyway, we stopped laughing about the whole car seat thing when Jason realized how incredibly complicated it was to install the first time. Don't feel bad if it takes a while. It took us only three hours to figure out.

The importance of asking for help . . .

When those well-meaning friends who love you say, "Hey, let us know what we can do to help," don't be afraid to be really specific with them. It's okay to ask for help. It makes everyone feel useful and a part of the experience. The same holds true for family members. If your baby is the first grandchild, the grandparents may need some advice as to how to be most helpful. For me, the best thing was food, and our family, friends, and neighbors were incredibly generous. Especially when you're breastfeeding, you won't believe how hungry you can get, and there's nothing like comfort food that you don't have to make yourself. And if you suddenly realize there's something you need that you don't have, by all means ask a friend if they can make a run to the drugstore or baby store for you.

No, your nipples can't fall off— it just feels like it . . .

So you have these two things on your body (your nipples) that you typically handle with care. Then, all of a sudden, you treat them to the suction of a human vacuum cleaner over, and over, and over again. Not exactly a recipe for comfort. You definitely want to have ointment handy for when the inevitable soreness and chapping occurs, but here's something else you can do: Get them ready. Just like an athlete going into training, you can start getting your girls prepared. I've known some moms who recommend using a loofah (gently) on their nipples in the weeks leading up to their due date. Other moms ask their partners to give the girls a lot of attention so they're a little more accustomed to the workout they're about to receive. Honestly? That sounds more fun than a scrub to me. Nothing is foolproof, but at least it's something. And either way, I promise you they won't fall off. Even if they bleed and you call the doctor thinking they are tearing off, they don't.

It's about nurturing . . .

Besides the sore nipples, I loved the time I spent breastfeeding my girls, and I was really lucky to have a pediatrician who supported me all the way. At a certain point, though, I wasn't producing enough milk for my little ones, so I had to switch to bottle-feeding. And I didn't beat myself up about it. When I was nursing and bottle-feeding, that time I spent nurturing my babies was beautiful, and I treasured every moment . . . even when I was half asleep. If you're having trouble with breastfeeding, I definitely recommend getting some help from a qualified lactation consultant (your pediatrician can give you recommendations). I will never forget the lovely lady who came into my hospital room like a mighty warrior and said, "Come on, let's get them ready." As she wrapped her hands around my breast to help me get my milk going, I couldn't help but smile. And as with everything, go with your gut and do what's best for you and your baby.

The top baby items you *really* need . . . or at least I did . . .

Of course there are a million things to buy for a new baby, from the absolutely essential to the unnecessary. I definitely recommend a less-is-more approach. Don't rush out and buy everything you can possibly think of right away. For the first few weeks, at least, you really don't need much. Everyone has their own personal list of new-baby must-haves, and here's mine:

1. Easy-access baby clothes—I wish I'd figured this out the first time, but it wasn't until I had my second baby that I discovered the joy of two-piece outfits and shirts with snap fronts—especially for those middle-of-the-night diaper changes. This way, when you're half-blind with exhaustion, you don't have to bend little arms, or pull shirts over their

heads (totally scary when you're a new parent). It also means that if it's just a dirty diaper, you can pull the pants down only as far as you need to, keeping the rest of your baby's body warm and covered. Of course my favorite baby clothes are from the Little Seed. I love putting my kids in organics since clothes touch their skin all day and night, and some kids, like mine, are more sensitive than others.

2. Wipes, wipes, wipes—You can never have enough. Ever. In every room of the house, in the car, in your purse, in your diaper bag, everywhere.

3. Disposable diapers—God bless those parents who use cloth, but for us, disposables were key. The natural-looking chlorine-free diapers were in our house for a very long time.

4. Burp cloths—For all of the spitting up your baby will be doing, and wiping that you will be doing, burp cloths are great. Cloth diapers can be great to use as burp cloths.

5. Soft blankets—You can have several of these and use all of them. Great for swaddling.

6. Pacifiers—They work when you need them, and I had no problem weaning. Well, maybe a little bit.

7. Baby caps and socks—Hats for sunshine in LA and for warmth in colder climates.

8. A place for the baby to sleep—Some parents use a crib right away, some co-sleep, and some use a bassinette at the start. Whatever your preference, have an idea of what you want to do in your head before the baby is born. It will make it easier on you.

9. A place to put the baby down—Bouncy seats, swings, or a Pack 'n Play are great for this. It's important to have a safe

place to put your baby when you need to take a shower or get something to eat.

10. Nipple cream—Okay, this one is really for you, but happy nipples make a happy baby.

11. A breast pump—Most moms can't live without them.

12. Diaper cream—Important for diaper rash, and a big must-have in our house.

13. A newborn kit—Including the booger sucker. There's nothing like your baby's first cold. The booger sucker has helped me many times.

14. Gripe water—A really great help on rough nights, if you have a colicky baby.

4

. . . .

Ya Never Know

Question of the day: When you were a kid, what did you want to be when you grew up?

"I wanted to be a doctor or a lawyer, a nice 'clean' job to make my parents proud . . ."

—Amelie

"A children's writer, a pastor, and Queen Elizabeth I."

—Amy

"A pediatrician, I wanted to help kids. Then I found out how much school was needed. Never mind."

—Joseph

"I remember wanting to be a nun til 6th grade; then Elvis's costar."

—Kathryn

"A mom :-) After that I wanted to save the world."

—Marly

can remember sitting around as a kid thinking about what kind of parent I would be someday. As I played with my newly adopted Cabbage Patch Kid, I just knew that one day I would have a baby exactly like my doll. I literally had an image in my head of a real-life Cabbage Patch baby. I had this view of myself as a free-spirited earth mother, flexible and loose, encouraging my kids to spread their wings and have amazing experiences.

I wasn't *completely* wrong in predicting future me. I was absolutely correct about at least one thing: I always thought the most important thing I could teach my children would be to *dream big*. And I still believe that with all my heart.

My own mother embodied that kind of optimism. I gave her plenty to worry about when I was little, but her hopes for me never dimmed. I didn't speak a word until I was three, and I know she had to deal with plenty of advice from people who thought there must be something seriously wrong with me. Then, on my third birthday, I spoke my first words: "Mom, how do you like my painting?" I can only imagine her relief at the time. But even years after that, I was still very shy outside of our family. Wherever we went I clung to my mother's legs, or hid behind my big brother Meeno.

It's interesting that a child as shy as I was would have been drawn to performing. But acting was a fantasy, an elaborate game of make-believe, and I loved everything about it. I tagged along with Meeno, who was a child actor himself, through back lots of studios, and soaked up everything from a safe viewing spot behind my mother's skirt. When I asked her if I could start acting, I suppose she could have gently steered me away—how was a child who was too shy to speak going to open up and perform in front of strangers? But my

Courtesy of the author

My mother, Sondra, and me when I was just a little baby

mom doesn't have a discouraging bone in her body, and I was a determined little kid. People always ask me what I'll do if either of my girls decides they want to act. The answer is that if my girls are anything like I was back then, I won't have any choice in the matter!

My mother, brother, and I were living in a little apartment in Los Feliz when I auditioned for the part of Punky Brewster. It was 1984. I was seven years old, and my brother

Meeno was thirteen. I will never forget all of us sitting and reading the script together. I fell in love with Punky from the very first moment. She was such a vibrant, spunky character, full of life, heart, and fun. And I dreamed of playing her.

The day of the audition, my mother and I entered the NBC studio and slowly rose in the elevator so I could meet my fate. The doors opened on the floor of the casting director's office and a little girl walked into the elevator with a smirk. "If you're here to audition for Punky," she said, "don't bother. I just got the part."

"Do you want to leave?" my mother asked me gently.

"No *way*," I said. "I'm going in there." The rest is history, and that moment of courage and dreaming big set the tone for my whole life.

My mother has always been an amazing parent. She was caring and constantly there for us, but she gave us the freedom to be who we were as individuals. Even if that meant making my Statue of Liberty Halloween costume out of tinfoil to be unique and within our budget, and letting me dress up and go to *The Rocky Horror Picture Show* at age eight. We ran

Courtesy of the author

Here I am back in the Punky days

through the grass in our bare feet, danced in the rain, and had chickens, bunny rabbits, and even a rescue horse named Butterscotch Freeway. We often slept outside. My childhood was magical. And it's all due to my free-spirited mom, a woman who traveled the world, had adventures, and gave birth to her oldest child in a windmill.

With that kind of example, I just knew the kind of mom I'd be—loving yet easygoing, attentive yet laid-back, loose and always flexible. And that's where my prediction of future me was just a little bit wrong. I've always taught my girls to dream big—always—and will continue to do so as they get older. But am I a laid-back hippie mom just like my own mother? Not as much as I had thought. Much to my shock, after going through a horrible case of reflux early on with Poet, I turned into a little bit of a crazy person—wipes were my constant friend. Shoes were removed at the door. Poet's pacifier was washed right away if it fell to the floor. I never dreamed I'd be so protective! But it just goes to show: You never know what kind of parent you'll be until you become one. Then the second kid comes along and you wipe the pacifier on your pants, and when they eat crayons you just figure they will poop it out. And that's why I try not to judge other parents. We all have an idea of how we will handle the screaming kid, the kid who won't eat, and the kid who won't talk. People certainly judged my mom all those years when I hid behind her. But Mom knew best—she always does.

When I had my first child, a lot of my friends didn't have kids yet. Now, in the last few years I've seen more of my friends go through the same things I did. They have their own ideas of what kind of parents they'll be, and often they sound a lot like I did when I was imagining my own future. My best advice to new parents is not to put pressure on yourself to be some ideal of the perfect parent. Share your ideas with other parents, and learn from them, but don't feel that there's any single right way to be a great mom or dad. There's a lot of judgment out there, and it can be really easy to get down on yourself as a result—or exhaust yourself trying to reach some unattainable goal. If you are happy, and your baby is thriving, then obviously you're doing something right.

I like to think I've now found a middle place between the mom I imagined I would be and the mom I turned out to be in those early days of having my first child. My kids and I run in the grass with bare feet, we dance in the rain, and one of these days (or years) I'll dress them up and take them to *The Rocky Horror Picture Show*. And when we get home, I can happily say that I will still ask them to wash their hands and take off their shoes before they go in their room.

* * *

S.P.S.

Looking in the mirror . . .

Write this down: Describe who you are as a parent—or, if you are pregnant, who you think you will be as a parent. Express the things that are really important to you and then revisit what you wrote down every once in a while. It is great to have a reminder of how we want to be and laugh at ourselves when we drift off. It is always good to look at ourselves in the mirror.

Holding on to the good stuff . . .

We can be so focused on the ways that we want to change when we become parents that sometimes we don't focus as much as we should on the things that really should stay the same. Before you ever became a mom or dad, there were things that were important to you, in a truly essential way. Maybe it was being playful with your partner, taking care of yourself physically, or expressing who you are through something creative. These are the things that help define you as a person. One of the most difficult things as a new parent can be feeling a little lost, like you're not sure who you are anymore. So make a list of who you were before you had kids. Now look at that list. Are you still that person? Have you lost anything really important along the way? How can you get it back? Share this list with your partner or a close friend. Help each other to hold on to the good stuff. Your kids will thank you for it.

Oh my God, I'm turning into my parents . . .

We've all had that moment when certain words come out of our mouths, and then we have this flashback to hearing our parents say the same exact thing to us. But it's not always a bad thing to turn into our parents in some ways, right? Here are some amazing things that my parents taught me about parenting:

- Encouragement—If I was passionate about something, then my mom and dad were behind me one hundred percent.

- Patience—I seriously cannot remember my mother ever raising her voice to me. How is that possible? Okay, maybe she raised her voice once or twice, but not very often at all. Such patience.

- Values—My parents separated when I was little, and neither of them had much money, so we learned that it's the quality of time and not material things that are important. They also always spoke kindly of each other, which I really respected growing up.

Courtesy of the author

My mom and dad cherry-picking on one of our awesome adventures

A little sentence to finish . . .

I know I've turned into my parents when I . . .

"Yell at my daughter to 'CLEAN YOUR ROOM!'"

—Sheila

"Say 'because I said so' as if it was a real answer."

—Kimberly

"Overly bundle up my children."

—Collette

"Tell my kids school is for learning not socializing."

—Nicole P.

Not-So-Traditional Traditions

Question of the day: What are your favorite family traditions?

"Pancakes on rainy days."

—Amy

"We have a few good ones. Amelia and I have mommy-baby yoga every day. We also schedule Play-Doh time. But my favorite is dinner on Sunday night. My husband and I take our little ones to our closest friends' house (they have a toddler too). We eat, parent talk, and enjoy the moments our little ones give us."

—AnaLiesa

"Watching football together through the NFL season."

—Annette

"My favorite family tradition isn't a set tradition, but whenever we get a chance, we make a small fire in the firepit in our backyard and roast marshmallows and talk. Even though our kids are young, they enjoy this time outside at night, and we hope to continue to build on this as they grow."

—JoyfulTxGal

"I love Christmastime and we have a bunch of good traditions surrounding it . . . cuddling up all together on Christmas Eve and reading "Twas the Night Before Christmas' right before we all go to bed. My mother cries every year reading it . . . Making a ton of cookies in the days leading up . . . Going to see a sappy movie on Christmas Day while the turkey is cooking and then my mom takes a nap."

—Kelly F.

My mother always says that she sleeps best when the house is full. The holidays are her favorite time of the year, when the whole family is under one roof. I am the same way. I'm never happier than when the house is full of laughter and joy—the more packed, the better.

When I was growing up, my house was everyone's home away from home. To this day, my friends remember eating my mother's home cooking and her always full house. On any given night, our dinner table would be crowded with Meeno's friends, my friends, and basically any kid in Hollywood who was in need of a home-cooked meal. Friends who were in town filming during the holidays were always invited over along with neighbors and extended family. The house was often packed. There were nonstop games of pool, and at Christmas you would even find Danny O'Connor from House of Pain and my other rapper friends singing carols and roasting chestnuts on the front lawn. Every Christmas Eve was filled with adventures and friends coming in and out of our house at all hours.

Courtesy of the author

My mom, Meeno, and me at the holidays

The holidays are my favorite time of year. I literally get excited six months beforehand. I try to conserve energy all year long so that I can light up the house at the holidays with a thousand twinkle lights everywhere. My husband shakes his head at how over the top with excitement I get about this time of year. So imagine my elation when we won Holiday House of the Year in our neighborhood.

It was a beautiful sunny day when I got the knock on the door. A person was standing with a bright smiley face as they shouted, "Miss, you have just won Holiday House of the Year." I jumped up and down and almost peed in my pants, I was so happy! They asked for the spelling of my name, and just as I was about to give it to them, my husband jumped in and asked what in the world I was doing. "Honey, we won an award for

Holiday House of the Year," I replied, sounding like a five-year-old who had just won a golden ticket to Willy Wonka's chocolate factory. My Jewish husband stared at me blankly before saying, "That's great, how 'eco' of you, and I'm sure my temple will be thrilled." And just like that, my crest had fallen. It wasn't enough that I had decked out our house with lights, angels, reindeer, and a golden gate, but to top things off, now we were winning an *award* for it. I kept that award certificate on my mantel for a year. Now we happily celebrate both Christmas and Hanukkah, and my husband has the wonderful name of Hanaclaus, for the tall and handsome Jewish Santa that he is to us.

Traditions are important in my family. We celebrated every type of holiday when I was growing up—Christmas, Hanukkah, Passover, Easter . . . as you can tell, my family was very open-minded. We believed in learning about other philosophies, and what better way to do that than to celebrate as many traditions as possible? One of my favorite memories was when I was about ten and we moved into a new neighborhood. My brother was going through his heavy-metal phase then. He had long, curly hair, and wore leopard stretch pants and ripped-up tank tops. I was always playing

Meeno

Jason and me on Santa's lap when I was pregnant with Jagger

dress-up—you would find me wearing all sorts of funky cowboy boots—and my mom looked like something between a hippie and a rocker. We had cars picking us up at all hours because I was doing *Punky* at the time, and we were often traveling. Anyway, it was Easter and we were in the middle of one of our big Easter egg hunts when the neighbors called the police. They thought we were hiding drugs. Between the way we dressed, the cars, and the wacky hours we were keeping, they were sure that our family must be connected to some illegal activity.

That is just how we rolled in my family, unorthodox and always breaking the rules, or at least breaking them while carrying on traditions. I learned how to ride a motorcycle before a bicycle and I got to stay up late as a kid and watch my two favorite television shows: *Dynasty* and *The Colbys*. I feel like I had a great childhood, even if it was a unique one. People often ask me how I turned out so normal. Normal? Hmmm. I'm not sure if I would categorize myself as one hundred percent normal, and I'm not even sure I'd want to. But I have a

happy and settled life, and I think more than anything it's because we always had such a sense of family. My mom made sure that we were able to be kids— and that our house was the place that everyone escaped to, not from. And as far as she was concerned, the more of us packed into that

Sondra Peluce

Me on an Easter egg hunt in my rockin' eighties clothes

house, the better. And just like all great traditions, they are meant to be carried on, and every day I try.

* * *

S.P.S.

Hanaclaus . . .

Of course, it's not that unusual anymore for families to celebrate multiple traditions in one household. I grew up learning about all kinds of religious traditions, and my husband, Jason, was raised Jewish. We were married by a rabbi and love to visit the temple. We teach our kids to be open to all religions. We also take them to visit churches, and have Buddhas and a Ganesh in our home. In our household, we have very happily merged Hanukkah and Christmas, and I once received some really great advice: So as not to confuse the meanings of different traditions, you can devote different areas of the house to the symbols of those celebrations. So, for instance, maybe your family room is where you put the Christmas tree, and the dining room is where you put the menorah. Whatever works and makes everyone feel happy and respected.

Celebrate a holiday your own way . . .

Who said that Valentine's Day has to be just about candy, hearts, and flowers? My brother and his amazing wife, Ilse, came up with a whole new way to celebrate Valentine's Day, and now we do it every year. We take the kids on a scavenger hunt through the city. My brother and his wife make up all the clues and fill a canister with treats, and then we go with the kids to look for treasures. This is a great way to explore the outdoors while taking the little ones on an adventure. Geocaching is also super fun and a great thing to do with the whole family. We try to do them on a regular basis. If you want to find more about geocaching, here is the website: www.geocaching.com. It's a blast!

Meeno

Our girls on one of their Valentine's scavenger hunt adventures

Not every tradition is a holiday . . .

I think it's incredibly powerful to have your own special traditions—things that you do together as a family. It really strengthens the bond. My husband had the amazing idea to designate Sunday as our family day. Every Sunday night we have a special family dinner and take time to talk about what we are grateful for. Sometimes we treat the girls to a special experience—like crab claws and Shirley Temples, which is so much fun. It is something that we all truly look forward to.

6

. . . .

Perfectly Imperfect

Question of the day: How are you most similar to and most different from your parents?

"I am the most similar to them because I have the same morals and values that my parents do. I rely on family and friends the most. I am most different from them because I am a younger mother and I feel that I am closer to understanding my children and remembering how I felt at their ages. I think this will make for a better relationship between us as they grow up."

—Jeannette C.

"I look like my mom and we have similar personalities. I'm impatient and disorganized like my dad. I voice my opinion more than my mom. I'm open-minded and a liberal, unlike my dad."

—Dana

"I am sensitive like they are, but since I grew up and moved out, I am not narrow minded, I know that we all come

from different walks of life and I try to be understanding
of others when our opinions differ."

—Irene

"I was one of those who said I was never ever going to be
like my mom but I can tell you . . . say it all you want she
is a part of you. My mom died in 2003 and I see a lot of her
in myself. It is just little things like the way she did things,
the way she moved or laughed."

—T Glass

I was five years old the first time I remember my father taking me to Iowa to visit my aunt Carol and uncle Mel. We
flew in very late, and on the way to my aunt and uncle's
house, we drove down a long highway. I was staring out the
back window when my dad started shouting, "Pull over, pull
over!" My aunt and uncle were perplexed as my uncle pulled
the car over. My dad pointed out the window at an old over-
grown graveyard. He turned to me and said, "You know
what that is, Soleil?" I replied, "No, Daddy, what is it?" My
father excitedly said, "It's a graveyard, want to go inside?"
Sensing my father's excitement, I said, "Sure." We jumped
out of the car as my aunt and uncle tried, with visible horror
on their faces, to stop my father. But it was too late—he took
my hand and we took off running through the graveyard,
chasing each other at midnight under a full moon.

My father was a real Renaissance man. He was an actor,
an artist, a four-time Golden Gloves champion, and, most
proudly, a civil rights activist. He, Marlon Brando, Paul Newman, and Tony Franciosa were known among many as the
Hollywood Four for their work together during the civil rights

movement. They went to Gadsden, Alabama, to fight for civil rights there, and then to the heart of Washington, D.C., to help lead the march on Washington with Martin Luther King, Jr. My father's charisma and open heart were abundant. He was also completely unpredictable and believed that rules were meant to be broken.

I loved spending the summer going on adventures with my dad to Iowa, where my aunt and uncle lived. We would eat corn for breakfast, lunch, and dinner, and watch TV at night until the national anthem came on and the screen turned to fuzz. While I remember the laughter most, there were some parts of our trips that weren't so funny. There was the time my father took me to the hair salon and decided it would be cute to make me look like Shirley Temple. So they put tight ringlets in my hair, and the curls stuck close to my head. It was horrendous. I looked more like a clown than Shirley Temple. My father proudly brought me home to my aunt, at which point I burst into tears.

Most of my time with my father was full of joy, though— and summer tornadoes. One of my favorite tornado stories took place during a different summer, when I had gone to Iowa with my older brother Sean (my father's son from his first marriage). Fifteen minutes after a broadcast of a tornado warning, my father had the bright idea to take us boating on the lake. My aunt absolutely forbade us to go outside. My dad never let a little danger deter him from what he wanted to do, so back and forth they argued until finally she gave in. I don't know why my poor aunt ever bothered trying to argue with him—she always lost. He convinced everyone to take the boat out, and there we were in the middle of the lake when the storm hit. The boat started spinning in insane circles, and the wind howled. My aunt was weeping and holding me like we were all going to die, my dad was laughing hysterically and I was laughing hysterically, and somehow we all survived.

Virgil Frye

Here we are on the boat in Iowa before the tornado hit!

It's probably obvious to you by now that my dad wasn't a father in some of the very traditional ways—he wasn't the one to pay for school or come at Christmas with loads of Barbies. But he was the one who would make the most unbelievable fudge, wrap it in foil, and bring it to us on Christmas morning. Or he'd go to a garage sale and find a tiny treasure that he thought I would like, or just show up with roses for no reason. At Halloween he would decorate our pumpkins with the most incredible, elaborate designs you've ever seen.

There was one time that my dad did a really traditional,

Sondra Peluce

Here I am with my dad and his amazing pumpkin masterpieces

fatherly thing. He took my best friend, Tori, and me to Disney World in Orlando, Florida. Somehow he'd gotten us full run of the park. He even found out that Jesse Jackson was there with his family, too, and we had an amazing, inspiring meal with them. Years later, I still have strong, fond memories of that idyllic trip.

My girls love Disneyland, and when I was there with them on a beautiful day a few years ago, I was just flooded with warm nostalgia for that time with my dad. And then I remembered something. I had a powerful flashback to that trip to Disney World, and to Tori and me pushing each other in a wheelchair. *Wheelchair?* I thought. Then I realized that when we got to the park all those years ago, my dad had taken one look at the crazy-long lines and then realized that people in wheelchairs got front-of-the-line access. That's when it hit me: Oh my God—my dad had gotten us a wheelchair so that we could cut the lines! It was so terrible that he did that . . . so totally wrong in every way. But twenty-some years later I still had to laugh at his wackiness.

I'm lucky that my mom was such a stable and reliable influence in my life—she balanced out all of my dad's unpredictability. They were together for only a few years after I was born, but they stayed friends and she always encouraged our relationship. And as a kid I truly loved his risk taking. Was my dad perfect? Not by a long shot. But somehow the combination of my more stable mom and totally unpredictable dad was just perfect for me. I remind myself of this when I'm feeling deeply imperfect as a parent. Thankfully, I'm not the only adult in my girls' lives—and Jason isn't, either. We've surrounded them with all kinds of people who love them in their own beautiful, quirky ways. Am I as adventurous as my brother Meeno? Nope. But I'm thrilled that my girls have an uncle like him. Am I as flexible and laid-back as my mom? Well, I aspire to be, but I don't always manage it. All of us together are my girls' family, so every day they get a wonderful stew of consistency and rules mixed with art, music, unpredictability, and lots of love. And that's what family is all about.

* * *

S.P.S.

Make your own adventure . . .

I think it's great to make day-to-day activities fun. Jason and Jagger absolutely love to do the food shopping together—it's become their weekly outing, and they both really enjoy that special time together. Sometimes when we go to the playground, we bring along a picnic, complete with blanket and basket to make it special. The little things can go a long way.

Exploring with our little ones . . .

We really like to take the girls out to explore. Maybe we'll go to a museum together, or take a bike ride at sunset, or roller-skate on the boardwalk. Something we want to do more of is setting up a tent in the backyard and camping. Of course we can do that in LA, where it's seventy degrees in the winter, but if you live in a colder climate, maybe your adventure is setting up a tent indoors or ice-skating. One of our favorite things to do is sledding—we love to get away to the mountains. Don't be surprised if years from now those out-of-the-ordinary moments become some of your kids' favorite memories.

7

. . . .

You Marry One,
You Marry the Tribe

Question of the day: What has been your most awkward in-law moment?

> "My in-laws are very cool, laid back, easy-going people. I am happy to report that there is not a single 'awkward moment' on record between us . . . thus far."
>
> —Amanda

> "My father-in-law's birthday dinner at Olive Garden. We weren't married yet, and had just found out we were pregnant. My mother-in-law knew right away just by looking at the way I was 'protecting my stomach.'"
>
> —AnaLiesa

> "When I thought my father-in-law was joking when he said he was Mormon, so I made a joke about it."
>
> —Dana

"The first time I met my mom-n-law. My bro-n-law tossed a ball @ me & I almost dropped it & said 'oh sh*t Timmy.' She later said she liked it cuz she knew I wasn't fake lol."

—Tracey

Here are Jason and me in the beautiful, tropical waters in Parrot Cay

It's all fun and games to talk about how nuts my family can be, but my husband actually has to live with these people, and it isn't always easy. Jason loves my family, but it wasn't until we had kids that it really hit him: My family was his family, too. *Oh my God.*

Superficially, Jason and I could not be more different. Jason: tall and acerbic. Me: short and sunny. Jason: raised conservative. Me: well, you know. But just as the weird blend of my parents worked out for me, the contradictory chemistry of Jason and me works for our kids.

Well, that's easy for me to say. For Jason, it was quite a bizarre and unusual learning curve.

When Jason and I got together, I was twenty and he was twenty-seven. I was living in a house with my mom and her boyfriend (whom she's since married). The first night Jason stayed over, I walked him into the backyard, and there was my bed—outside. To me, this was totally ordinary—I loved sleeping outside. Of course Jason was immediately convinced that my family was scamming me out of all my *Punky Brewster* money, and I wasn't allowed a bedroom in my own house.

Eventually Jason suggested we sleep in an actual room. One night, we were in bed, it was two in the morning, and my mother walked right into our bedroom and shook me awake. "Honey, turn on the TV!" Then she started flipping channels until she found a show featuring a televangelist named Benny Hinn. She was beyond excited, because she had submitted a prayer for me, and Benny Hinn had just recited it on TV. Then my mom put her hands on the TV, and she sighed with happiness. It was right about this time that Jason decided we should get our own place.

And so we moved into an adorable little Spanish-style one-bedroom apartment, and eight months later, we were engaged. One afternoon, about two months from our wedding day, we had just gotten back from a meeting with the rabbi at Jason's synagogue when my mother called. "Jason," she said. "You're never going to believe who's in town—Benny Hinn!" Then she begged Jason to get us tickets to the show. He couldn't bear to disappoint her, so he called the number my mom gave him and was relieved to get the voice mail. He left a message, assuming we'd never hear back.

Within minutes, of course, they called—Benny Hinn would *love* to have Soleil Moon Frye come to his show! And that's how, just hours after meeting with the rabbi who was going to perform our wedding, my mother, my Jewish fiancé, and I went to a Christian revival meeting along with 55,000 other people. The arena was vibrating with energy, and we were seated right in front. My mom was chatting away with everyone in our row, and I was having the time of my life—I loved all the good vibes! It was awesome. Jason was looking at his watch and praying that no one would ever find out about this.

Then Benny Hinn came onstage, resplendent in his white suit, and the show started—and lasted for four hours. Toward the end of the show, spotlights started circling the audience, and Benny Hinn said, "We have a special guest here tonight— I'd like to welcome Soleil Moon Frye! Soleil, why don't you come on up here!"

While Jason was thinking, *No, no, no, no, no,* my mother was saying, "Yes, yes, yes, yes, yes," and pushed me out of my seat. "This is a blessing," she said. "You'll be able to touch him!" So I went up onstage, and I don't know what came over me, but when Benny Hinn asked me what brought me there that night, I grabbed the microphone and yelled into it, "HAL-LELUJAH!" And then 55,000 people yelled, "HALLELU-JAH" right back at me. So I grabbed the mike and said it again. And happy hordes yelled it back again. By this time the house was coming down with excitement, Jason was terrified that somehow his rabbi would find out about this, and my mother was beaming with joy. I was riding on a high of happy energy, so I grabbed the mike again and I yelled, "PRAISE THE LORD!" I was just in the moment, going with the flow, and the energy of those 55,000 people was *awesome*. Then Benny Hinn said to me, "I'm going to heal you," and I said back, "HEAL ME!" So he touched me on my forehead, and next thing I knew, I was flat on the floor.

Jason was stuck in his seat with no idea what to do about his unconscious fiancée. In a minute I was back up on my feet and escorted back to my seat. What happened to me up there? I haven't the foggiest.

Finally, four hours into the show, the spectacle ended. Before Jason could shove us out the door, a guy came up to us and said that Mr. Hinn wanted to see us. Jason said, *"NO!"* My mother said, *"YES!"*

Next thing we knew, we were in Benny Hinn's private quarters, and he was handing out blessings. First he put his hand on my mother's head, and boom, she was down for the count. Then he put his hand on my head, and down I went. Last, it was Jason's turn. Hinn put his hand on Jason's head, and . . . nothing. Hinn squinted at Jason and cocked his head slightly.

There are times in our lives when we have to make a defining decision. For Jason, in this moment, the decision was: Is this my family, or not? Am I truly one of them, or am I going to slide out that door and wait for these lunatics in the parking lot? Jason, bless him, decided to stick around. And so there was only one thing for him to do in that moment. Benny Hinn's hand on his forehead, Jason went down for the count—fully conscious.

And to that I say: HALLELUJAH!

* * *

S.P.S.

The joys of family by marriage . . .

I know we sound a little eccentric—and we are—but I think part of what brought Jason and me together is that we are such opposites; and as wild and crazy as we can be, we are a family. A colorful and unique one. I didn't grow up with a sister, and I feel so blessed that my brother married such an amazing woman—Ilse. One of my big joys in life is when Jason and I go out on a double date with Meeno and Ilse. We get a baby-sitter and the cousins all stay together and have their own movie night. I know that having this closeness—both for us and for the girls—is so awesome in our lives.

Let's hear it for grandparents . . .

What would we do without grandparents? I didn't grow up with them, although I had an amazing god-grandmother named Jackie, and Jason's grandmother became one to me. But I didn't have what my kids have. I feel so blessed that our kids have awesome grandparents. And I know a lot of people really see their own parents with new eyes when their parents become grandparents. All the baggage of our childhoods can fall away when we learn just how hard it is to be a parent, and how much they love our kids—and how much our kids love them.

8

Please, Sir, May I Have Another?

Question of the day: What did you do to prepare your older child for the arrival of a new sibling?

"Have them talk to the baby and love on the belly continuously."

—Collette

"My son was only a year and 5 months old, and is Autistic, so we tried to talk to him about his sister that was on the way, but he was not old enough to understand. If he were older, I'd involve him in getting the baby's room ready, buying things for the baby—just making him feel involved and important. And I would assure him the baby wouldn't affect my love for him."

—Sheila

"I involved her in as much as possible. Dr visits, baby shower, etc. I made sure to show her and tell her that I love her at every possible opportunity. I explained that even though there will be a new baby, that I love her the same as always—more and more each day, but I would have to give the baby a lot of attention for a while. After her sister came, I involved her in diaper changes, baths, feedings, etc. so she wouldn't feel as left out and ignored . . . and gave big praises for her help."

—Dana

"I made a big deal out of what a cool thing it was to be a big sister—I was one, after all. Not that she agrees at this point . . . lol."

—Cari

I always wanted a big family. I remember being really little and telling my mom that I wanted to have a hundred kids. She told me to be a teacher. Now, of course, there are some days when I feel like I can barely handle the two kids I have. Other days, especially when I hold my youngest and I realize how big she's getting, I want to have more.

Poet was just about two when we got down to business and decided to have another baby. I'd heard all the stories about older siblings who wanted to send the baby back when they came home from the hospital. *Yikes*, I thought. I really didn't want that to happen.

So from the very start we set out to make Poet feel totally included. We told her the news right away, and we let her know that as the big sister she was really, really important to this baby. We all talked about our favorite names, and Poet was constantly talking to the baby in my belly.

The last few weeks of my pregnancy were this incredibly defining experience for our little family. I slowed down to be with Poet—totally and completely, with no distractions. We walked around the neighborhood and looked at butterflies and trees. We got ice cream and took our time eating it. We smelled the flowers. We cuddled close and talked about the baby coming. My godmother, Patricia, came to stay with us, and she showered both of us with attention. It was a totally magical time that set an amazing tone of love and welcoming.

Patricia Hanwright

Poet and me enjoying the moment together as we waited for Jagger's arrival

Jagger was born two weeks late, on March 17, 2008. Once again I had my playlist and my sheets from home, but this time I added a picture of Poet to my room at the hospital. The Soleil Moon Frye Birthing Team was back together again— Demi was a coach, Tori was right alongside her, and so were my mom and godmother. The whole room vibrated with music just the way it did when Poet was born.

After Jagger was born, we just wanted to get home. We didn't even take the time to bathe her in the hospital! Jason brought Poet to pick us up, and the look on her face was this amazing mixture of shock, awe, and pure love at first sight.

We wanted to keep that loving feeling going, so at home, we included Poet in everything. Jason and I each had our special moments with Jagger—she was this little Buddha baby, totally peaceful. And when one of us was with her, the other one was focused on Poet. Three days after Jagger was born, she stayed with my mom for a few hours while we took Poet to see the trains in Griffith Park. It was one of our favorite places to go before Jagger was born, and we wanted Poet to know that the world she knew before wasn't closing down— it was just getting bigger and more colorful.

A few weeks later, Jason was working in San Diego, and I took Poet to LEGOLAND and the San Diego Zoo. It seems totally crazy now that I look back on it—I'd just gotten rid of that beautiful mesh granny panty and ice pack combo, and I was running around an amusement park already. What was I thinking?

But it was worth it. Our crazy campaign worked, and Poet

Suzi Haydon

Here I am with my two little girls; I couldn't be happier as our family grew.

felt very special and included. We made Jagger's arrival into such a joyous celebration that Poet welcomed her sister with open arms. And we all learned that our hearts just keep on expanding with our family, and there's no limit to how much we can love.

* * *

S.P.S.

Making way for number two (or three, or four) . . .

There are all kinds of ways to include older kids in getting ready for a new sibling. One of our favorite things to do with Poet was baby naming. We would come up with fun ideas together. Poet also helped me with picking out clothes for Jagger and giving her the things that she had outgrown. The most important times are those precious weeks before the new baby comes. It is such a great time to bond and share your love with your kids. Also, you can let them come up with fun ideas that they want to do with the new baby, like planning an outing the first month. Art projects are another wonderful way to engage your older children. They can help decorate the baby's room and make it special. If your older child is losing some space to the new sibling, try making them a part of the new design. They can help you pick out fun paint colors or new toy bins. Another important thing for us was reusing with our second baby. Half of Jagger's things in her room—her dresser, armoire, and clothes—came from Poet. There's nothing more eco than that, and it is also far more affordable than buying all new stuff.

Plan activities for after the baby comes . . .

Before the new baby comes, ask for your older child's help in coming up with some fun activities that you can do together—with just you and them. This way your older child has some one-on-one time to look forward to and they can see that their interests are still really important to you. Maybe it's a play-date with their best friend, or a trip to their favorite park or beach—or a combination of all of the above. No matter what, make it something special and out of the ordinary, and all about the older sibling.

A little sentence to finish . . .

When I brought my new baby home from the hospital, the first thing my older child said was . . .

"That's not our baby. Our baby in there (patting my stomach)."

—Genie

"When is the baby going back in your tummy? I want my lap back."

—Carrie

"I want to hold him!"

—Amy L.

"Could he go to the bathroom?"

—Alea

9

. . . .

Trusting My Gut, and Not the One I Came Home with After the Baby

Question of the day: When has following your gut gotten you into or out of trouble?

> "I followed my gut by deciding not to further my education beyond 2 years of college (and no degree). I am happy to be where I am now, but I think I could have seriously benefitted from a good education. The best part is that you are never too old for education!"
>
> —Amanda

> "Too many times to recount. I trust my gut, my instincts. I've learned that as a mom, it's the one thing you should always listen to!"
>
> —Jeannette C.

> "Following my gut actually has always gotten me out of trouble for my entire life. It is when I second guess that feeling that I actually get into trouble!"
>
> —Luna

"Co-sleeping. I cannot get her out of my bed now without her KNOWING it. However, I have faith that she will fall from the apple tree eventually. I actually believe that co-sleeping will prove to have GREAT benefits in the future."

—Natalie

People ask me all the time what it was like to work from such a young age. The truth is acting never felt like work to me—especially not on *Punky Brewster*.

That set was our home away from home, our school, and our playground all rolled into one. The other kids on the show and I would ride around the lot on our scooters, we'd pogo-stick around the *Santa Barbara* set right next door, down the hallways, off of furniture, and through the makeup room. It was so much fun, and it never felt like work.

When I wasn't taping *Punky*, I attended a free-spirited private school that was all about hands-on learning. I went there from preschool to junior high. I became a total mad scientist in sixth grade, thanks to my amazing science teacher. When we were dissecting rats in school I got so attached to mine that I named it Mellow Yellow. My teacher let me bring the rat back to the *Punky* set with me to show everyone. I then took it to my friend Cherie's house for a sleepover that night. I forgot to tell Cherie's mom that I'd stuck the formaldehyde-soaked rat in her freezer, so when Mrs. Johnson reached in for a Popsicle later that night and came out with Mellow Yellow instead, she actually fainted. Oops.

That same science teacher taught us how to grow wheat, and then how to make alcohol from the wheat (and if we had a note from our parents, we were allowed to bring a sample home). I loved chemistry, so my teacher supplied me with ingredients to take home and experiment with to my heart's content. I gathered all our neighbors around, mixed judicious amounts of sulfur and magnesium together, and blew up a nearby manhole cover. It was a huge hit on our block.

I hope my girls get to learn from someone brilliant just like my science teacher, maybe minus the vodka making. He inspired me and all of his students to go out and follow their passion, and that's the kind of parent I want to be. Poet loves performing, so we give her every opportunity to dress up and express herself. Jagger's a little comedian—so who knows, maybe she'll grow up to do stand-up. Or not. Wherever their passions lead them, we want to be there telling them to go with their gut and do what they love.

I think a big ingredient in good parenting is having the confidence to follow your gut, and the flexibility and courage to let your kids follow theirs. I was inspired to follow my gut by the unique people in my life and also from my mom, who could have discouraged me from pursuing my dream of acting, but instead went with her gut and let me go with mine.

Thanks to her, I got to know myself really well, and I've always been able to stay true to myself and what's best for me. I remember when Jason and I got together, we were such opposites. When we told my mother that we were getting married, she said we'd be lucky to make it ten years! She has never lived that down, but I definitely don't blame my mom for being worried—I was only twenty-one years old, and although my mom loved Jason, she felt like we were so young. I was still her baby, after all. But thankfully I followed my heart (just the way my mom raised me to do), and I knew that Jason was the one.

For me, parenting has been the same—I believe in

trusting my instincts, and so far they haven't led me wrong. When Poet was really little, she was incredibly shy (like mother, like daughter). She had so many fears. Fears of people, places, and things—especially fireworks. To this day she has incredibly sensitive ears. I suppose we could have pushed her into situations where she'd have to learn to adjust to new people and big sounds, but trying to negate her fears just never felt right to me. In my heart I knew that when the time was right, she'd get past them.

Just last week, we went to Disneyland with the girls and my nieces. My nieces are older than Poet, and I could see Poet wanting to follow them onto the bigger, scarier rides. And then the moment of truth came—Space Mountain. I kind of looked at Poet sideways to gauge her response. She said she really wanted to go, and I thought—*all right, if she says she's ready, then she's ready.* And she absolutely loved it. Then, right after she got off the ride, the fireworks were about to start. I told her that we could stay inside and she could cover her ears. She looked at me and said, "Or maybe I could go out and watch them and maybe I'll be okay." And she did—and it was.

Courtesy of the author

Our big family at one of our favorite places in the universe, the magical world of Disneyland

There I stood, watching my daughter dance with her cousins under the crackle and boom of the fireworks. She had found her way through her fears, just like my gut told me she would.

* * *

S.P.S.

Listening to your gut . . .

Sometimes we want to help our kids make good decisions—or we want to make good decisions for them—and it feels like our heart and gut are telling us one thing, and our brain is telling us another. If our kids tell us they don't want to try something new—maybe a class or a sport or even a new food—we're not sure if we should push them to do it, or if we should let them be. I've learned that sometimes the best way to figure this out is to really listen to your children. Then ask questions, and really listen to their answers. When kids say they don't like something and don't want to do it, sometimes it just means they don't like one part of it. And if you find out what that is, you can ease them through it instead of giving up on the activity altogether. For instance, Poet loves her dance class, so I was surprised when she came home from class one day and said she didn't want to go to dance class anymore. So I kept asking her questions, and I really listened to her, and finally, after a long heart-to-heart, it came out that she just didn't like the style of dance that they were doing for a few minutes at the end. Kids can often see things as black or white—"I love it!" or "I hate it!"—and sometimes they need our help to see the gray areas. Once I reassured her that I would talk to the teacher and that she could sit out that part of the class if she really wanted to, she was fine, and back to dance class she went. The next day she was dancing her heart out and even joined in at the end. She just needed to be heard and understood. Sometimes all they need is for us to listen—really listen.

Follow their passion . . .

Is there anything more amazing to watch than a kid who discovers they love something new? It's such a joy. You may not be able to send your future astronaut to the moon, or take your little marine explorer scuba diving, but there are lots of ways to encourage our kids' interests without breaking the bank. Poet has started really loving math, so at dinnertime we'll go around the table doing simple math problems. And a trip to the library is the cheapest way of all to encourage kids' interests. If you have a kid who loves music, let them play with your iPod and make their own playlists. Pretty soon you'll want them to make playlists for you. And if you have a budding artist, make sure that they have a little spot all their own to make masterpieces without worrying about making a mess. Because following your gut can get messy—but it's so worth it!

10

. . . .

Expect the Unexpected

Question of the day: Was there one specific parenting moment when you realized it wasn't going to be as easy as you thought it would be?

"When my son was diagnosed with autism, and all the challenges that brought, that definitely showed me being a parent was NOT going to be a walk in the park at all times."

—Sheila

"There wasn't a specific moment, but more of a realization that I was spending more time washing clothes and cleaning up the house than anything else."

—Ashley

"Giving birth."

—Nicole P.

"Breastfeeding for sure!!"

—Collette

"Colic. I think I cried as much as my daughter did."

—Cari

still remember the romance of my honeymoon. The beautiful waves, the tropical setting . . . the hurricane evacuation. Let me back up.

Jason and I had originally wanted to go to the Caribbean for our honeymoon, but it was hurricane season, so everyone advised us against it. And we listened! We're not crazy—we wanted calm seas and warm breezes. That seemed like a lovely way to start our life together. Our rabbi suggested Mexico, and we thought: Perfect solution. We're there.

Our wedding was beautiful, a stunning affair! After the

Meeno

Our wedding day—truly one of the happiest days of my life

reception there was just enough time to pack up and go to the airport. I remember being on the plane, and how excited we were to be beginning this amazing new chapter in our life together. We were full of optimism, radiating happiness like light.

When we landed, we thought, *Wow, it must have been a really popular time of the year to travel to Mexico.* There were thousands of people in the airport waiting for flights out, wall-to-wall travelers and luggage. Somehow we managed to miss the signs of panic in the air—maybe due to our newly-wed bliss. The greeter for the hotel seemed a little odd and kind of half-smiling as he packed our bags into the van, but we didn't take much notice of that, either.

As we drove to the hotel, though, we got a little more observant. "Wow, it's kind of cloudy," I said. "Wow, it's kind of windy," Jason said. Meanwhile, tiles were flying off rooftops, and the trees were being blown perpendicular. All the greeter for the hotel would say was "Oh, it's just a little bad weather."

Yeah, it was a little bad weather, all right. It was Hurricane Mitch, the most powerful hurricane of the 1998 season, and by the time we'd driven a little farther through vacant streets lined with boarded-up buildings, it became clear that there was a full-on evacuation under way. When we got to the hotel, the only other tourists left were a couple of seventy-year-old storm chasers, and the waves were so high that they were actually crashing against the glass doors of our hotel room.

That was it for us. We rushed down to the lobby and said we wanted out—immediately. Anywhere in the world. The first available flight was going to Mexico City the next morning. We reserved our seats, and we headed back to the airport to wait it out along with all the other storm refugees we'd passed on the way in.

And that's how it was that my perfect wedding was officially consummated in a tiny Mexico City airport hotel room.
My godmother told me later that I should consider myself
lucky—not because we survived Hurricane Mitch, but because
a disastrous honeymoon trip was a very good omen for a long
and happy marriage. So far, it seems like my godmother was
right. My own personal theory is that our honeymoon is just
one more example of fate laughing at our best-laid plans. We
flew away from a hurricane . . . into a hurricane. Of course!

Life keeps teaching me to expect the unexpected. I can
try to predict the likeliest possible scenarios, but I know it's
just a matter of chance as to whether I'm right or not. I know
that if I'm flying with my girls, it doesn't matter how much
I've packed in my carry-on, it will turn out that the one thing
I didn't pack is the one thing I need. I also know that even if I
changed a diaper right before we got on the plane, the second
we're up in the air and the fasten-seatbelt sign is on, my kid is
going to poop. And there's not a thing I can do about it but
smile, deal with it, and pretend we're all somewhere else, somewhere peaceful and quiet.

I remember the first time I thought Poet had seriously
injured herself. She was a year and a half, running around the
hallways of Jason's office, and she fell. It was her first knot
on the head, and I freaked. I thought the world was ending.
We took her straight to the ER and called the pediatrician
from there. His words were something like "What are you
doing in the ER? It's just a knot." Just a knot? Just a *knot*? Oh.

None of the usual clichéd parenting advice could possibly
prepare me for the realization that I will never stop worrying
about my girls *for the rest of my life*. And I have story after
story of close calls—enough to keep me awake for years. Like

the time when Jagger was two years old and escaped from a hotel room in Washington, D.C. She was riding on the elevator downstairs, all alone, when my husband found her. And I will never forget the day I got a call from Poet's preschool telling me that she'd fallen on the playground and severely cut herself right above her eyebrow. Our doctor sent us to a pediatric plastic surgeon right away (a brilliant piece of advice that made all the difference), and he did a beautiful job. Not only did he pick me up when I saw the cut for the first time and almost passed out, but he was so gentle and caring with Poet. In future years Poet will no doubt enjoy comparing her scar with all her friends' scars.

What I've learned from these and other similarly insane incidents is that I have *so* much less control than I ever thought over what might happen in my kids' lives. Each scary experience stops our hearts a little bit. No matter how hard we try to protect our little ones and keep them safe, they will end up with their own scars and scraped knees.

*   *   *

S.P.S.

What to do in those heart-stopping moments . . .

What do we do when we get one of those calls that stops our hearts, or we see our kids walking in with blood on them from a big fall? Take a deep breath and try to stay calm. Of course, I am also the mom who has panicked a hundred times, but I try my best not to. I nearly passed out when I caught sight of my daughter's injury from the playground. But I definitely learned from that. Something else I learned? It's amazing what a difference a fun bandage can make. Our girls have a tendency to get really upset at cuts and scrapes, so we keep them distracted by whatever cool bandage we have in the medicine cabinet.

You can't predict everything that might happen. Even if you tried, chances are that life would still throw a surprise at you. So plan in advance as much as you can. Keep your pediatrician's number in your phone, some ice packs or frozen peas in the freezer, and a first aid kit in the medicine cabinet. Take a CPR class or two like I did (yes, I'm a crazy mom who took two), and make sure your home is a safe place for curious little ones.

After you do all that, you'll still worry, and you might even panic now and then. It's the nature of being a parent. The good news? We're all in it together.

What goes in my carry-on when traveling . . .

- Gum, lots of gum. Poet has super-sensitive ears, so having fun-flavored gum really helps.

- Books and a few toys. I let the girls help pick out a few of their favorite things from home to bring with them. This way it is not too much stuff, but they feel connected to what they are bringing.

- Mama's first aid kit in case of emergencies. I made it myself. It has all of my must-haves: Band-Aids, etc.

- Wipes. I always find myself needing wipes for them and for me. Our last flight, chocolate M&M's had melted underneath where the girls were sitting and you could see me scrubbing the seats with wipes as everyone was leaving the plane. It was a lovely sight.

- A change of clothes for both girls along with a hoodie or something warm in case they get cold.

- Writing books and crayons for them to draw.

- Snacks. Fun snacks that you all love and can enjoy together. I don't know what it is about flying, but the minute I am up in the air, I am starving.

Finding the right pediatrician . . .

We're incredibly lucky that we found the perfect pediatrician for us. I know for myself that I need a lot of hand-holding. I also like to have a doctor who I can talk to openly and on a regular basis. And our doctor is comfortable with that. When you're interviewing pediatricians, think about the connection you want to have with your doctor. Always ask the questions close to your heart. I'm a firm believer that there's no such thing as a stupid question, and I don't think your pediatrician should ever make you feel bad about asking. Most important, trust your gut, and when in doubt, get a second opinion.

11

. . . .

What's Yours Is Mine

Question of the day: How do you best handle sibling rivalry?

"Having a large family (seven children at home), sibling
rivalry could easily get out of hand, but honestly it's an
easy one for us and doesn't happen very often in our family.
If a sibling hurts another or is saying mean things, the
offender spends the day serving the one they hurt. They
must play with the one they hurt and let them pick the
activities. The offender will also take care of their sibling's
chore as well as serve their meals, get their drinks, etc.
Our goal is to not only 'pay restitution' for their offense but
to also help teach how your actions create reactions and
consequences."

—Retta

"We have three of them and sibling rivalry seems to work
in our favor. Two of them will always gang up on the third,
but you never know which two it will be! Recently my wife
and I had to talk to a clerk at a sales counter. We told our

9 year old to watch the other two. Five minutes later they were both sitting perfectly still and quiet. We asked our 9 year old how he did it and he said, 'I told (the 4 year old) I had a job for him, which was to watch (the 2 year old) and make sure she didn't get off the bench, because she'd be in trouble if he told me. Then I told her the same thing.'"

—Allen

"Sibling rivalry is best handled by doing your best to assure your children you love them all the same and that everyone is unique and different and not everyone may be treated the same all the time, but the love is always the same no matter what. Even when you do not get along with your sibling love them as you want them to love you."

—Paul

When I was born and my mother brought me home from the hospital, my big brother Meeno took one look at me and said, "Can brothers marry sisters?" Somehow, I was blessed with a sibling whose heart was so open to me that we were close from the moment I entered the world. Meeno is six years older, and in a lot of ways he's been more than a brother to me. He was like a second father. My mother worked so incredibly hard to support us, all on her own. When she couldn't be there, it was always Meeno. He changed my diapers; he tucked me in at night. He walked me hand in hand to my first day of preschool, and when I didn't want to be alone at night, he let me sleep in his room.

I would love for my girls to have just that kind of relationship, but of course they're a lot closer in age than Meeno and me. They love each other and they have great times together,

Sondra Peluce

Here I am with my big brother, who really helped raise me. He was my big brother, a second dad, and my best friend.

but they also drive each other crazy. Poet adored her baby sister from the start, but it got a little harder once Jagger was old enough to take her toys away from her. Then things got a little more challenging.

I know the whole sibling thing gets to be tricky at times. At least in our household it does. When the girls are fighting over something, sometimes I don't even care what started it. I just want them to stop arguing. On a few occasions, I actually bought two of everything just so the girls wouldn't fight over what belonged to who. If one got a coloring book, I would try to get the same coloring book for the other. If Poet was drinking from a pink cup, I would try to get the same cup for Jagger. Then I realized that even when there were two identical items, they would still manage to argue. One would decide that the identical thing that her sister had was better than her own in some way. I remember thinking early on in my new-mother bliss that when I had kids they would never fight. I would shower them with so much love that they would never feel the need to compete for my attention. Looking back, I just have to laugh at myself. Aw, the joy of thinking I could always make everyone get along. The reality of having two kids turned out to be totally different.

One day I must have been right at the breaking point,

because I just sat in the hallway of the girls' school thinking about all the ways I was surely screwing up my kids. When Carol, the head of our school, caught sight of me, she sat down and got the gist of my dilemma. She asked if she'd ever told me the shoe story. I looked at her sideways. "The shoe story?"

Carol said, "Soleil, when one of your kids needs shoes and you take them both with you to shop, do you buy each a pair of shoes or only the one that really needs them?" I admitted that I usually bought both a pair, because I didn't want the other sibling to feel left out. Then Carol said an amazing thing, and it has truly changed my life. She pointed out that while I was trying to keep the peace by giving the same thing to both girls, I was actually taking attention away from the child who really needed it in that moment. Meanwhile, I was also not allowing the other child to be a part of helping her sibling. I swear, my head started to glow like a lightbulb. It was so simple, and it made such perfect sense.

The next week it was raining in Los Angeles, and Jagger needed some rain boots, so both girls and I went shopping. There we were at the store, and of course Poet saw a beautiful pair of pink rain boots that she wanted. But Poet didn't need rain boots—she had a pair at home. It was Jagger who needed rain boots. In the past I would have broken down and bought that pink pair for Poet, too, but instead I thought about Carol's advice. I gently took Poet aside and said, "Honey, you already have rain boots, and this is your sister's first pair. Can we make it special for her?" She looked at me with bright eyes and said, "Sure, Mom." Then we excitedly rushed over to Jagger and helped her put on her new rain boots.

Now, I'm not saying that this strategy will work every

time. But it's certainly worth trying. Almost everything is worth trying when you want to help your kids get along. Sometimes we just need to separate the girls—Jason will take one of the girls to go do something, and I'll take the other. But that's not always possible, and there are plenty of times that no matter what we do, the girls fight. And then Mommy curls up in a corner and cries. Not really—but sometimes I want to!

Thankfully, there are other times—quiet times, when neither of them realizes that anyone is watching. I quietly stroll by Poet's room, and there she is, holding her little sister in her lap. Their love for each other is so genuine. At moments like that—no matter how many arguments there might have been during the day—I know we've done something right.

Soleil

My two little girls in the crib together. One of their favorite pastimes: playing in the crib instead of sleeping in it.

* * *

S.P.S.
. . . .

Be my little helper, please . . .

Ever since we first brought Jagger home from the hospital, we've included Poet in helping to take care of her. It has always empowered her and made her feel proud of being a big sister. So when the two of them are fighting over something silly, or maybe Jagger is having a hard time finding something fun to do, I'll ask Poet to help me out. From the time Jagger was a newborn, I'd ask Poet to please grab some wipes for me, or bring a diaper for her baby sister. Now, I might ask her to draw a picture with her sister because she is such a great teacher. It might get me only a few minutes of quiet before they're screaming at each other again, but I think it's good for our kids to play an active part in keeping the peace. It also creates an incredible bond, and they are protective of each other while being both nurturing and still having a sense of independence.

Let's all just get along . . .

I wish I could say that I have found one strategy for smoothing out all sibling conflicts. Life would be so much easier! Sometimes the best way to make sure your kids don't fight is just to give each one a little space and alone time. There is a really great way to make sibling reunions sweeter, though. Sometimes when I have something special to do with one of my girls, we will make a point of bringing something home for the other sister. And it's important to let your child pick what that is—it should be their gift to their sibling. It doesn't have to be a big deal—a sheet of stickers or a ball. The key is that one sibling is doing something nice for the other, and they get to see how great that feels. And it makes them want to do it more often!

Sticky situations . . .

Poet takes a great theater class, and last week Jagger was invited to attend the class with her big sister. Jagger was so excited and she just loved it. Unfortunately, the next week there wasn't enough room in the class for Jagger. She was crushed. I was at a total loss for what to do. Should I take both girls home and wait for a class when they could go together? I didn't think that would be right, because it was a class Poet had signed up for, and she shouldn't have to miss it. So we explained the situation to Jagger in a way that she could really understand, and—miraculously—she was cool with it. And she happily watched while her sister took the class. Amazing! Sometimes a little compassion for our kids can go a long way. Sure, lots of sibling conflict is over silly things like who gets the pink cup and who gets the purple cup. But often there's a real reason for the conflict, and while you might not be able to completely fix the situation, you can listen and respect your child's feelings. The outcome can often surprise us!

12

Don't Speak to Me Like That

Question of the day: How do you encourage open communication among members of your family?

"We have a chalkboard in our kitchen and this is where we encourage everyone to write whatever is on their minds for the whole family to see. I find that this brings positivity in our household, while solving any issues that might be circulating among the children."

—Ashley

"In my family, honest opinions and thoughts can be hidden behind humor. While I try to allow the humor, I also take the time to get behind it and find the true thought."

—Jill H.

"No matter how busy our week gets, we sit down AT LEAST once a week for a meal together and talk."

—Amy L.

"We never let anything slide. We're such an open family
that everyone feels comfortable enough to say what they
need and want to."

—Nicole A.G.

Once our kids get past the baby years, we're confronted
with an amazing—and scary—prospect. Those infants
who weren't able to do anything without our help can suddenly talk, and walk, and do plenty of other things without
us—and without our permission. And when that happens,
we as mommy or daddy, who were so used to being nothing
but one hundred percent supportive all the time, are faced
with being . . . disciplinarians. You can definitely add that to
the long list of things that I never expected to be when I
grew up. But as a mom I've learned that discipline isn't a bad
word. I'm the least rigid person on the face of the planet, but
still, we all need some rules to live by.

I'm lucky enough to be able to spend a lot of time with my
kids. I work from home, and even when I'm juggling ten different things, my kids are right there. It's wonderful! And I'm
so fortunate! It's also *exhausting*.

I'm also incredibly lucky to have a supportive and totally
involved spouse. As parents, I think we agree about the really
important things, but sometimes our parenting styles are just,
well, different. Jason is more of a daredevil, and the girls love
that. At the end of the day, he swoops in from work full of fun
energy. I want to go with the flow and just be happy that the
girls are happy, but sometimes I feel like the bad cop to his
good cop. When they're racing around the house or jumping
on the beds, I'll admit that I'm kind of losing my mind.

It's a little easier to be good cop when you work outside the home, and you've missed most of the daily meltdowns. Just the other day, Poet was exhausted and inconsolable. It was that point in the evening when it's not quite time for bed yet. I've noticed the girls' emotions can be very close to the surface during that time. And of course that's when I'm also tired and my patience is on its way out the window. Anyway, Poet really wanted her daddy—*now*. Jason was working late, but finally, Poet seemed so upset, I decided to call Jason to see if he could come home and help out. By the time Jason got home, Poet was fine, the crisis was over, and he kind of wondered why he'd raced home. I tried to explain that as calm as things might have seemed when he walked in the door, not a half hour before, all hell was breaking loose.

That situation was a good reminder to me that a lot of times, when the girls are at their most difficult to manage, it's not because they're being defiant—it's because they're tired. I was frustrated trying to get Poet to relax, because I was trying to fix whatever problem she was having—instead of realizing that her biggest problem at that moment was that she just needed to go to sleep. I've learned, through a lot of trial and error, to try to give them a little room for their emotions when they're exhausted like that.

Weekdays can be tough. The kids have full days, and Jason and I are each running around doing our best to manage work and parenting, but weekends are when we all get back on the same page and remember that we're a team. During the week we might be Mommy the disciplinarian and Daddy the daredevil, but when the weekend comes, everything evens out. We're both with them all day, every day, and we get to appreciate how each of us contributes. And every once in a while, Daddy gets to play bad cop, and Mommy just smiles.

* * *

S.P.S.

When you're having a tough time and nothing else seems to work, draw it out . . .

I can't remember the first day Poet said, "Don't speak to me like that," or rolled her eyes at me, but I am pretty sure I was in complete shock. Now I try to remind myself to breathe as she is having her five-going-on-fifteen moments. Heart-to-heart talks are great, but when our kids are having a hard time articulating how they're really feeling, I will ask them to draw it out. Rather than send the kids to their rooms to calm down, I'll ask them to draw me a picture about how they are feeling. I give them a piece of paper and some crayons or pencils and let them put all of those overwhelming emotions down on paper. It gives them a safe place to put their feelings, no shouting needed. It has really worked wonders. We look at the drawing when they are finished and we talk about it, and usually all of us are coming from a much calmer and happier place.

13

. . . .

Eating Dessert First

Question of the day: What is your favorite dessert to make with your kids?

"Homemade waffles with fresh fruits."

—Mary

"A trifle—it's so easy and fun. You make the chocolate devil's food cake and let the kids help you layer the Cool Whip, cake, pudding, berries, and fruit."

—Hillary

"Birthday cakes for the people we love. The kids love to get the decorative icing and draw themselves. Plus, there's something insanely cute about 'Happy Birthday' written by a 3 & 5 year old!"

—Jennifer

"Homemade cookies. It may sound simple, but with a 3 year old rolling dough with a pin and my 10 year old decorating it's hours spent in the kitchen baking and cleaning flour off the kids' noses."

—AnnaMae

My mom was a food artist, and my earliest memories all involve food in some way. I vividly remember her cleaning shrimp in one side of the sink while I sat in the other. She came home from events with lobster tails and salmon, and our perfect dessert was a massive bowl full of Queen Anne cherries, eaten outside. Meanwhile, my dad's side of the family—the Nashville side—stuffed me with fried chicken and corn three meals a day—it was *heaven.*

Sondra Peluce

Here I am covered in eggs. My mom let me wear my food while I ate it, which was one of my favorite things to do as a kid.

I don't remember any food ever being forbidden when I was a kid. Food was a good thing, something to enjoy, and there was nothing negative about it.

And thankfully my kids love to eat everything—Indian, Japanese . . . and cupcakes.

The other morning I took the girls out for breakfast, and Jagger really wanted a red velvet cupcake. So I figured, why not, and I got cupcakes for both of the girls. While we waited for our eggs, Jagger dug into her cupcake right away but couldn't get past three bites. Poet decided to save her cupcake for later. My friend Stephanie walked over, took one look at my girls with their cupcakes for breakfast, and she laughed teasingly and said, "What's for dessert?" A few minutes later she watched in amazement as the girls sat gobbling up their eggs and toast—and veggies, too.

I guess what some people would call being permissive, I call being flexible. Of course, we don't eat a bag of M&M's before dinner, although I have been known to give the girls one or two when they ask. My belief is that food is like anything— try to deny your kids' impulses too long and eventually they're going to blow and probably go overboard in indulging.

Some of my favorite memories from childhood are the special treats my mom would put in my lunch box. It might be a candy ring, or a candy necklace. Then one day she put something *really* special in my lunch box. Right around that time there was a launch of a new alcoholic beverage that was packed, conveniently enough, in containers that looked exactly like juice boxes. My mother grabbed a six-pack of those fruit-punch boxes, not realizing that the second ingredient was vodka. She sent it in my lunch box the next day. I pulled it out, and my teacher grabbed it right out of my hand and called my mother. Poor Mom; I can only imagine how she explained that one away.

Of course, I'm not recommending we all stick booze in our kids' lunch boxes! But I do think a treat now and then is a fun way to get our kids to look forward to their lunches. Creating healthy eating habits is all about giving our kids a healthy balance. We wear organic clothing and go to the local farmers' market often, but we also have gummies in the cabinet—and our friends' kids who don't have any sugar at home all want to come over to our house. I have a friend whose son refuses to eat anything vaguely unfamiliar. He came over recently and I convinced him to try a "surprise smoothie." The surprise ingredients, known only to me? Avocado, broccoli, and chocolate ice cream. He loved it. It helped that it looked (and tasted) more like chocolate ice cream than broccoli, of course.

I try to make food as fun and exciting for my girls as my mother did for me. A few weekends ago my kids and my nieces decided they wanted to make a candy cake. By the end of it, there was candy everywhere, and the cake was way too sweet to eat—even for the kids—but they had a blast. Another fun thing we do is a game I call Mystery Eating Experience. During these experiments I have the girls close their eyes, give them little tastes of food, and have them guess what they are eating—an olive, a piece of cheese, a chocolate-covered pretzel, one jelly bean.

I'm not saying that cupcakes for breakfast are always a good idea. Or that you can cure a picky eater with a blind taste test or a particularly fun mealtime experience—but it couldn't hurt to try. And if it takes spoonfuls of chocolate ice cream to make the broccoli go down—whatever works for you!

* * *

S.P.S.

. . . .

Making it fun . . .

I'm a big believer that food and eating should be fun. And one of the best ways to have fun with food is to enjoy a variety of

tastes and textures. I was told by a friend that one of the reasons American kids tend to be much more picky as eaters is
that we give them blander foods than other cultures, so strong
flavors and spices can taste weird to them. I'm lucky that my
girls are good, diverse eaters, and one of the things I do to
mix things up and keep it fun is to make a platter of little
dishes of things. So when we're watching a movie, instead of
a big bowl of popcorn, I'll put a whole bunch of things on a
tray—a small bowl of Pirate's Booty or Smart Puffs, five or
ten chocolate-covered cranberries or yogurt-covered raisins
in another dish, some cut-up apple in a bowl, plus slices of cheese,
some crackers, a few strawberries or sliced grapes, and a little
saucer of olives. I know it may sound crazy, but it's fun to have
choices and options, and it's also kind of festive and makes a
snack into something special.

Lunch box ideas . . .

A friend of mine gave me the best idea for making lunch boxes
more fun. I saw her making her daughter's sandwich and cutting it into fun shapes with a cookie cutter. Her daughter was
a tween at this point, and my friend had been doing it for her
since she was little. The daughter never wanted her mom to
stop doing it for her because it made her feel so loved. So I do
the same thing for my girls, and it really does encourage them
to finish their lunches. Here are some other ideas for making
lunch boxes fun:

- Sometimes I leave notes and drawings in their
  lunch boxes (I'm hoping this won't be embarrassing for them as they get older).

- A little sweet something, maybe a granola bar they love. The other day I put a few gummy bears in Poet's lunch and she actually came home and told me not to do it anymore, because "it wasn't healthy." I say there's nothing wrong with putting a special treat in there now and then if it makes them excited to open their lunch box.

- Dips! Kids love to dip—so try carrots or celery with a little container of hummus, cream cheese, or their favorite salad dressing.

- Have them help make their lunch—kids have so little control over their lives, and just like us, they like to eat what they're really hungry for. So put the lunch stuff out on the counter and let your kid help choose. If the morning's a rush (and what morning isn't?), do it the night before.

- Pack mini-bites—kids love a little of this and a little of that. So give them a little bit of several different things (cut fruit, a string cheese, some raisins). This works especially well for younger kids who like to graze.

Little chefs . . .

I love cooking with the girls, and I've learned a few tricks for how to make it fun and relaxing for me as well as for the kids. First, it's really important to put things on their level. So in our kitchen we have a small table and chairs where they can sit and stir or decorate our latest creation. When I'm making salad at the counter, I have them stand on a chair next to me, and after I cut the vegetables, they put them in the bowl and mix it up. And believe me, kids are a lot likelier to eat a salad that they've helped to make. Here are some of my other favorite things to make with the girls, and yes, we love dessert:

- Breakfast—Pancakes and waffles are so much fun to make and great for teaching measuring and a little math along the way. It's a great place to start with aspiring cooks.

- Cookies—Again, easy, fun, and a great way to involve the kids in the recipe. Let them choose their add-ins. My niece Bindi had the great idea last weekend to add mini-marshmallows to our chocolate-chocolate-chip cookies.

- Cakes—We love to bake cakes. We make them together, and our favorite part is decorating. White cake with pink icing and sprinkles is very popular in my house right now.

Baking therapy . . .

I don't know what happened, but recently I started baking like crazy and now I can't stop. There's something about the moment the heavy whipping cream turns into peaks, and pouring the sugar into the measuring cup while the sun shines through the window. It is literally like therapy. My husband looked at me today in total disbelief after I had made a strawberry pie, banana bread, and two different chocolate-chip-cookie recipes. Of course, our kitchen looked like a tornado hit it, but truly I have to say I have found such joy out of baking. And the fact that I get to do it with my little ones makes us all happy. So next time you need to get something out, instead of screaming, crying, or heading to the gym (although I should probably do that one of these days soon), I say put on some of your favorite tunes and bake like crazy. Let the flour fly and the vanilla drip, and just let go and have fun.

14

. . . .

What's in a Name?

Question of the day: What is your all-time favorite name?

"Maggie."

—Stephanie

"Cassandra."

—Jeannette C.

"Ophelia."

—Dana

"Sophia."

—Natalie

My family has always loved unique names. With names like Soleil and Meeno, my big brother and I cherished our individuality. Between me, my brother, godbrother, extended family, and friends, we all carried on the family tradition.

Since I was a little girl, people have asked me about my

name. Soleil means "sun" in French. One of the inspirations for my name came from a song my mother loved from *Annie Get Your Gun*—"I've Got the Sun in the Morning (and the Moon at Night)." As a little girl, I was so happy to hear the story about how I was named—and how my mom thought her baby daughter was the sun and the moon. I've always wanted my girls to feel just as happy with their own names. I wanted them to know that there was no one else on earth just like them. My father wanted to name me Megan, but at the end of the day, my mom won the name battle.

I was only six weeks pregnant when we first thought of the name Poet, and we immediately liked the idea that we could call her Poe for short. But we didn't quite settle on it at that point. Then it was Father's Day, and Poet was due in a few months. We were walking around in Santa Monica thinking, *What are we going to name this baby?* We were in a little shop and we looked up to see a framed quote by Edgar Allan Poe: "All that we see or seem is but a dream within a dream." And right next to that was a mug that said, "Poet." It felt like she named herself. Poet's middle name was inspired by a cathedral in Siena, Italy, where I'd said a little prayer before I got pregnant with her. And she had two great-grandmothers—one on either side—named Rose. And there she was, our Poet Sienna Rose Goldberg.

With Jagger, I remember she was so strong in my stomach and she would give me the hardest kicks in the world. I knew she had to be the strongest baby—she felt like a boxer! She was a little Jagger from conception. Then it was funny, because she was born with the most peaceful demeanor. She was just so calm and easy, a Buddha baby. But oh, all that strength was underneath. As soon as she could walk around and assert herself, we were like, oh yeah, she's a Jagger all right!

Jagger's middle name, Joseph, came from my godfather, who had passed away the year before she was born. He was the patriarch of my family—he'd been there when I was born, and he walked me down the aisle when I was married. We wanted him to live on in our family, and naming Jagger after him felt like the most natural tribute in the world. Then we came up with her other middle name—Blue—just because we loved it so much.

There are whole blog posts devoted to wacky Hollywood names, and a few of those have definitely mentioned our kids, but in my family, unconventional names are the norm. My brother's name is Meeno, and he literally named himself. My mother lived with him in India when he was little. He was a few years old, and one day as they were hiking, a monk asked his name. My mother said, "Miro" (his given name), and he turned and said, "No longer Miro; now Meeno." So Meeno it was. His girls are named Bindi and Mette. We've got my god-brother, Joachim, his sons, Orpheau and Jobim, not to mention other wonderful wild names in our family. So Soleil, Poet, and Jagger are just more entries in a grand family tradition. When my friends and I sit around talking about names, we turn to everything for inspiration—literary references, favorite places, special family members—whatever is truly meaningful to us.

Now that my girls are five and two, I like to think that they're the perfect embodiments of their names. But the truth is, they could have the most traditional names in the world, or the most unusual. And no matter what we named them, they'd still be utterly unique and completely themselves.

* * *

S.P.S.

Everyone's got an opinion . . .

Some people choose to keep their baby names a secret before giving birth, and others decide to share it with the world. Just remember that people will always have an opinion. It would be great if all those opinions were nothing but positive, but the fact is that they won't always be. So just be prepared . . . and if people say, "How interesting," just smile and say, "Thanks, I think so." Not that I am speaking from personal experience or anything. :)

Keeping a list . . .

I love coming up with baby names. It is one of my favorite things to do. I have friends who walk around with lists or keep names in a secret diary—even the ones who don't have babies yet. It is awesome. A really fun thing to do is to keep a little journal. When you are inspired by something or someone, write it down. Then go back and add to it from time to time. I still have names that I came up with when I was twelve. Don't be afraid to be imaginative and to have fun.

A little sentence to finish . . .

If I could go by any name other than my own, it would be. . . .

> "When I was younger I wanted my name to be Samantha. Now I'm happier with my own name."
>
> —Sherry

A family of wacky names: Mette, Meeno, Soleil, Poet, Jagger, Bindi . . . and Jason

"Isabella."

—Carrie

"Natalia, the name that my father wanted to give me, but my mother won that one. I am now Nicole. . . eh, still an N person. :o)"

—Nicole A.G.

"Mommy is just fine :)"

—Amy L.

15

. . . .

Happy Birthday

Question of the day: What was your favorite birthday party ever?

"When I turned Sweet 16! I woke up to 16 balloons in my room, and later had a wonderful party with lots of friends and family. It was still the best one yet!"

—Jeannette C.

"The only sleepover I ever had. My mom rarely let kids spend the night, so it was a special treat to have several over at once."

—Dana

"My daughters' 13th dance party in my garage."

—Natalie

"When I turned 16 and my parents had a surprise party for me and they invited a bunch of my friends and we played volleyball and went swimming and had a BBQ."

—Yolanda

"My favorite party was when I was 18, but I'm still young and I expect to have another great one when I hit 30 and 60 and 90!!!"

—Tazia

Just like holidays, birthdays have always been incredibly important to me. To this day I can remember almost every birthday celebration I've ever had. And it's not about the presents. What I remember most is how my mother showered me with attention, made my favorite foods, and always made me feel special and loved.

For my sweet sixteen my mom had the awesome idea to have a reggae bash. She rented a party boat that would take us around Marina del Rey, and she thought it would be really cute for me to stand at the front of the boat as it pulled in to the dock, where all of my friends would be waiting for me. Try to picture this: me waving to everyone I knew, decked out in all my teenage glory. One of the highlights of my life is when I bump into my friend Kevin Connolly and we burst out laughing, remembering how ridiculous I looked standing there in the bow of the boat, in my skintight cherry-red dress and cowboy boots, waving to everyone. In retrospect, it is hilarious.

Another birthday that stands out was my twelfth. It was a big party, and the last season of *Punky*—a huge milestone in my life. I was dressed in the coolest eighties trends—hot pink lace bloomers under a black spandex dress with hot pink polka dots. The hotel banquet room was filled with pink balloons, and everyone was there—family, and friends I'd grown up with in and out of the business. I was laughing and hugging everyone, and then in walked my special surprise: Johnny

Depp. He was starring in *21 Jump Street* at the time, and I had met him a few times before. We shared the same publicist, Jeff, who knew what a massive crush I had on Johnny, so this was his birthday gift to me. He came to the party with his buddy C. Thomas Howell. I still remember what Johnny was wearing: a yellow shirt and gray jacket. I'm pretty sure that a twelve-year-old's birthday party in a hotel banquet room was not Johnny's usual scene, but he was totally sweet about it. We were surrounded by kids, and photographers were all lined up in front of us, and after a while I could tell that the guys were ready to leave, but the route out was blocked. So I grabbed each of them by the hand and said, "Follow me!" While my friends watched in total surprise, I led Johnny and C. Thomas Howell through the crowd and out of the banquet room, and

Jeff Ballard Public Relations

Here I am with the gorgeous Johnny Depp and C. Thomas Howell at my twelfth-birthday party.

went running through the halls of the hotel, down steps, and down more halls and stairs, and finally all the way down to the lobby, where I located a bar. How did I know at age twelve where the bar was, or that these guys would appreciate being led there? I don't know. Let's just say I was precocious.

After the party, my brother Meeno loaded me and a few of my friends into his black Camaro (the height of cool at the time), and we listened to Lenny Kravitz booming from his car stereo while he drove us up into the mountains. He'd bought us some cherry-flavored cigars (I know—disgusting), and we sat perched over the city, puffing away. I probably threw up after the cigar, but the night was perfect.

I want my own girls' birthdays to be just as perfect, minus the cherry cigars. One year I made Poet's birthday a little *too* memorable—for the dads, anyway. It was a Tinker Bell–themed party, and let's just say that the Tinker Bell I hired was very pretty and really filled out her costume. It's no surprise that the next birthday characters were two people dressed up in Mickey and Minnie Mouse suits. Unfortunately their car broke down in front of our house, so my lasting memory of them was Mickey and Minnie waiting for a tow truck.

For Poet's fifth birthday, we had a *Grease* birthday, and it was a blast. We had the full fifties theme with makeup stations, dress-up stations, and of course a dance party. And just so Jagger didn't feel left out, we made her the party host. She greeted everyone, and then at the end she got a special gift from the birthday girl. And we do the same when it's Jagger's birthday. Poet is the host. Because the last thing you want at a birthday are hurt feelings. Or hot Tinker Bells.

* * *

S.P.S.

Fun ideas . . .

Even elaborate birthday parties don't have to be expensive. For our *Grease* party, I went online and found discounted Halloween costumes and spandex pants. A friend set up the makeup station, and another friend sprayed the girls' hair into wild fifties styles. And a dance party costs nothing if you're willing to play DJ. Here are some other fun ideas:

- Do-it-yourself goodie bags—Fill mason jars with candy, and give each of the kids a rubber-stamp-decorated brown paper sack to fill with candy to take home.

- Fairy/treasure hunts—This is one of my favorite things to do at birthdays. Throw a bunch of fun goodies in a bag, and then put them all over the yard or park and the kids can go find them.

- Crafts—Buy a bunch of inexpensive frames and let the kids decorate them with paint, stickers, and glitter.

- Giving back—Planning a birthday that connects kids to giving back is amazing. Talking to them about bringing toys for kids in need and taking action is a great way to raise children with a sense of compassion and awareness.

Remember that it's not a competition . . .

We all want a happy birthday boy or girl, but it's important not to compare ourselves to other people. I've never seen a kid who wasn't happy just to get together with their friends and eat some pizza and cake. Sounds like a party to me!

Prepare the birthday boy or girl . . .

Lots of kids—particularly the little ones—have breakdowns at their birthday parties. I will never forget the one birthday when Poet cried as the cake came out, and it broke my heart. It's good to sit down and have your kids be part of the planning process. Poet and I had a blast on her last birthday putting out the candy and coming up with the cake she wanted. She loves party planning.

Involving siblings . . .

I really believe in involving siblings in the process. Poet and Jagger are already talking about plans for Jagger's next birthday. They are picking out themes and music. I love hearing them talk about it with such excitement. I feel like the more they can help each other, the more supportive they are in celebrating their birthdays.

A little sentence to finish . . .

The best present I have ever gotten for my birthday was. . . .

"A clean house."

—Ash

"Sheets with teddy bears on them, because when I pointed them out to my dad I swear he was not listening!"

—Jeannette M.

"My first Easy Bake Oven. The best gift that I have ever received as an adult for my birthday was a pair of tickets to see *Wicked* from my other half. And you think they don't pay attention at times. :o)"

—Nicole A.G.

"A Walkman for my eleventh birthday. My Dad was a musician and that was the year I really started getting into music so he got me the Walkman. He passed away a few months later, but I'm glad we got to bond over something that was so important to him."

—Sheila

"An ice cream bday cake—those were A-list back then."

—Mikala

"Waking up to a homemade baby bassinet in my bedroom made by my mom with all matching bedding she sewed and a sweet baby doll inside. I will never forget it."

—Collette

"A green and yellow bicycle for my 7th birthday . . . I had
wanted it so badly and have never forgotten it!!"

—Betsy

Suzi Hayden

Poet and me dressed up as Frenchie and Rizzo at her *Grease* birthday
party

16

. . . .

Yes, Michael Jackson
Was My Babysitter

Question of the day: When trying to find a babysitter for your children, what do you look for most?

"I have a special needs daughter (7 yrs old) so I only let my mom watch her, or a friend's 17 yr old daughter who I've known since my daughter was 2 yrs. old. She knows all of my daughter's needs. If I were to look for another sitter, it would be someone who I think is trustworthy, responsible and who will play with Sade and not just sit there and play video games and text all night."

—Becky

"I look for people I know and I trust can handle my kids. Four is a lot against one."

—Carrie

"I look to the girls that work in our nursery at church, or that work with my mother-in-law at her daycare."

—Amy L.

So there I was sitting with Michael Jackson, alone in his Jacuzzi, talking about life, love, and the secrets of the world. I was eight years old. Yes, I know you are probably horrified, or at least a little confused as you read this, wondering how in the world I got there, so let me take you back a few weeks.

Two weeks earlier my friend Kidada Jones invited me to go to a Bruce Springsteen concert with Michael Jackson. Her father, Quincy Jones, and her family were very close to Michael. So there we were on the *Punky* set when the limo pulled up. My mother, Kidada, and I jumped in and were off to see Bruce. We were sitting in box seats when Michael walked in with the most glamorous woman I had ever seen. She was stunning, and her name was Elizabeth Taylor. Michael was kind and soft-spoken. I gave him a gold yo-yo as a gift, and he played with it under the table for the rest of the night. Elizabeth Taylor wore an enormous emerald ring, and I asked her if she had gotten it from a candy machine. She smiled at my naïveté. The night was fun, and at the end, Michael invited us to come over to his house sometime.

Two weeks later my mother and I were eating vegan tomato soup in Michael Jackson's kitchen. He was dressed in his famous red coat and white glove as the three of us sat at a table. My mother spoke of her travels to India and living in an ashram as he told us about his healthy eating habits. Bubbles, his chimpanzee, joined us throughout the evening. Michael took my mother and me on a tour of his home. We saw his elaborate costumes encased in glass, his bedroom, all of his knickknacks, and his stunning recording studio. Later that evening, Kidada joined us. Her father was there recording with Michael, and my mother had to leave to work on a party for Dennis Hopper. They were going to screen *Willy Wonka and the Chocolate Factory* in his movie theater later in the evening, and I begged my mom to let me stay. My mother finally said yes, and there I was exploring the candy station at his ranch in North Hollywood.

We watched *Willy Wonka*, and Michael and I sat next to each other. He had a way of speaking as if he were a child, too. I remember him leaning in, our heads close together as we whispered and giggled. After the movie, Kidada left, and it was just Michael and me. He then said, "Come on, let me show you the animals." We went outside on his stunning property and began walking over a bridge when a swan jumped out at me. Michael threw me to the ground in an effort to protect me. He explained that the female swan was pregnant and so the male swan was protecting her. Seemed normal, I guess.

We saw his beautiful llama and then went back to his house. It was around this time that he went to change Bubbles and I found myself alone in the foyer of his mansion. All of a sudden on the intercom I could hear Michael saying, "I see you." I looked around, for the first time feeling slightly uneasy, trying to figure out where the sound was coming from. I think once he realized he had freaked me out, he came out to get me. "Want to take a Jacuzzi?" he said. I replied, "Sure." I was excited and thought it would be fun. I remember having a hard time finding the right bathing suit, but I finally settled on a dark green one.

So there we sat in his Jacuzzi, talking about life. As I mentioned earlier, even at five, I wanted to know people's entire life stories. I was eight then, so I asked Michael plenty of questions. I remember him talking about the fact that he related more to kids than adults, and that grown-ups never completely understood him. He sat across from me and we had a dialogue as if we were peers—a true heart-to-heart. He never made me feel like this was a bizarre situation. It just seemed as if he really wanted someone to talk to, someone who would make no judgments about him. After the Jacuzzi we went down to the arcade and played games until my mom came to pick me up. Michael never left my side that night, and when we parted, he was very kind. I never saw him again after that, and I am not sure that I even told my mom about the Jacuzzi until recently. This story is not one I have shared often, but now I realize, if even for only one night, Michael Jackson was my babysitter. As strange as it all sounds—and I know it sounds strange—it was a highlight in my young life.

Recently, I was in a situation where I really needed extra help. I had a big meeting and found myself locked out of my car down at the beach with the kids. I called everyone I knew and trusted but couldn't reach anyone. My husband was able to get me halfway to the meeting in his car, but not all the way due to his own hectic schedule. The only person I could get ahold of was my Teamster stepfather, Shawn. He and I had a strained relationship over the years, but he was immediately ready to help me. Jason pulled into the parking lot of Yum Yum Donuts, and I jumped out of our car with my two girls and into Shawn's giant gray truck. We were off to the Valley, where my meeting was. I ran into my meeting frazzled, but when I came out, I found my stepfather pulling up with my happy girls in tow, holding on to Slurpees. They also were holding signed head shots of the Laker Girls. Apparently, the Slurpees were free because, according to my five-year-old, "The Laker Girls let us spin the wheel." I looked at my step-father, wondering what 7-Eleven he had taken the girls to. His response was "One that had Laker Girls." Fair enough, I suppose.

When we got back to my house, the kids were happy, and Shawn stayed for dinner. As we sat around the table, chatting and feeding the girls, I realized it was the first time that he and I had ever been alone with the girls. Suddenly our not-so-close relationship became so much warmer. The one person in my family that I would never have thought to depend on became someone I really needed to depend on, and our total dynamic changed. What a gift. In that moment any frustration that I had with him as a stepfather disappeared because I saw the incredible grandfather he had become, and my heart opened up in a way I did not realize was possible.

One piece of advice I can give from this experience is to write down a list of the people you love and you really trust, keep that list by your side for emergencies, and even add the ones you might not usually think of, because you never know when you are going to need that one person you might never expect. I don't think my mom ever imagined that the King of Pop would be my babysitter. Just like I didn't know my Teamster stepdad would be a big teddy bear I could totally count on.

* * *

S.P.S.

It takes a village . . .

It can be really hard for us to imagine that anyone can take care of our kids as well as we can. I know lots of parents who never go anywhere without their kids because they haven't found anyone they trust. Sometimes, this fear isn't really about our kids—it's about us. It's also important to remember that our kids learn really important things from people other than us. My kids get totally different—and wonderful—things from their grandparents, friends, and the other amazing people in our lives. And experienced babysitters or good friends can also empower our kids to do stuff for themselves that maybe we always do for them without even thinking about it. As my mom always says, "It takes a village." I really believe that, and I'm grateful for the friends and family who surround us and our girls.

Knowing when to ask for help . . .

I have learned to ask for help when I really need it. This has not always been easy. Of course I want to be supermom and do it all. Write, design, pick up groceries, drop the kids at school, pick them up from school, make breakfast, pack lunch, make dinner, run a business, the list goes on. For any parent, we do our best at artfully juggling life and family while trying to balance it all. Now I ask for help when I really need it without being hard on myself. Often my mom is here playing with the kids on the floor or making a beautiful art project outside while I am writing. Then I get to swoop in like supermom and really enjoy their artwork or roll around on the floor with them. It's good for all of us! So don't be afraid to ask others for help. You can still be a superhero while leaning on that village.

17

· · · · · · · · · · · · · · ·

What I Learned from Punky

Question of the day: How do you encourage your kids' quirks?

"Let them decide what they like and what they don't. Schedule time for things like digging in the dirt or dancing in circles. Save old clothes for playing in the rain. Have towels for wiping off mud. (Can you tell I have boys?)"

—Allen

"Just let them be. Don't draw attention to them and don't try to get rid of them. If they are quirks to stay and part of them, they will withstand the test of time."

—Hillary

"Be involved!!! My 3-year-old son is very much into how things work, so we take apart the controllers, cover off the computer, etc. I want him to know that questioning how things work and why is a good thing! Never settle for the big picture! My 5-year-old daughter likes to put makeup on herself and pick out her clothes. Instead of telling her she looks silly (but in a very cute, silly way), I tell her how glamorous she looks and then I ask that she make me up and pick out my clothes. :) It's fun one-on-one girl time for us and has given the UPS man quite a few laughs when he drops off packages!"

—Jennifer

"I was the anti-princess mom. Then Cortana said to me after I dressed her one day, 'Look mommy! I look just like a pretty princess!' . . . Now she has a princess kitchen, a princess bed, a treasure box of princess dress up, and princess clothes AND shoes. She also loves pirates so we're hoping for a well rounded, butt kicking princess. :D"

—Kelley K.

"Let them express themselves, within limits of course, if they are not harmful to themselves or others, there's no need to point out that they are different. Just let them be the individual they were created to be."

—Whitney

When you play a character for as long as I played Punky, sometimes the line between where you end and your character begins can get kind of blurry. For me, Punky was so much like me, and I was so much like Punky.

Punky had her own unique sense of style and so many great crazy catchphrases. Now I can't remember if Punky said them first or if I did. Some of my favorites were "Holy macanoli," "Grossaroo," and of course *"Punky Power!"* I still laugh saying that. In fact, I laughed hysterically when I decided to dress up

Decked out in all my Punky glory as an adult.
I really do love laughing at myself.

like Punky to celebrate getting my one millionth Twitter follower. I went full-on Punky in pigtails, rolled-up jeans with a bandana around one leg, bright mismatched sneakers, the works. My daughter said, "You can't dress like that, Mom!" (Ah, the joy of embarrassing my children.) It was *so* much fun to get into that character again, after all these years. Once I started yelling "Punky Power!" it was hard to stop.

Even before "Punky Power," the world of acting was the perfect place for a kid like me—it played right into my two biggest personality traits at that point. The first was my incredible curiosity. I always wanted to try everything, see everything, taste everything. My big brother regularly had to stop me from trying to eat bugs and dirt. And my other biggest personality trait then? Let's just say that I was a little . . . quirky.

For example, I loved horror movies as a kid. I inhaled horror films like other kids watched cartoons. I was just six years old when I got my first opportunity to be possessed by the devil, and I dove in headfirst. The movie was Wes Craven's *Invitation to*

Hell. I used to love sleeping over at my friend Cherie's house because her mom would let me rent the most gory, scary movies. I would stay up at night watching them by myself. So a movie like this was a dream come true for me. The morning of my big possession scene, I woke up and I wouldn't speak to my mother, I'd only give her freaky stares.

Courtesy of the author

As a little girl, quirks and all

I guess I was Method acting or something, getting ready for the scene where I was supposed to stab a stuffed bunny rabbit with a crowbar. My big line, spoken in a gravelly, "redrum" kind of voice, was "Bad bunny, bad. Bad bunny, bad."

Another of my quirks was actually caught on film a few times. For at least a year when I was about five, I was compelled to say the word "probably" after every single sentence I uttered. This is literally how I spoke: "What's going on, *probably*? I really love you, *probably*. Please pass the potatoes, *probably*."

One of my first speaking parts was in a TV movie called *Who Will Love My Children?* I was the youngest of ten kids whose mother (played by Ann-Margret) was dying of cancer. In one really intense, emotional scene, Ann-Margret was crying and I was sitting on her lap eating ice cream. I was supposed to look up at her and say, "I want to go to heaven with you, Mommy." I said my line perfectly, but if you look really closely, I think you can see that I'm mouthing the word *probably* at the end of my moving little speech. Thankfully, acting eventually broke me of my "probably" phase.

It was fortunate that I ended up on a show that was all about curious kids finding their way in the world and learning from their mistakes, and the writers and directors loved to pull plotlines straight from the stuff that was happening in our little-kid lives. One of the first times that happened was right after the *Challenger* disaster. Everyone around me knew that I wanted to be an astronaut. When I got to my school on the set that horrible morning of the explosion, a few of the kids told me, "We'll watch your family for you if you die." I burst into tears and carried that sadness with me for days. The result was a visit to the *Punky* set by Buzz Aldrin, and an episode in which he encouraged Punky to keep following her dream of becoming an astronaut.

One of the most popular episodes we ever made was when Cherie got locked in a refrigerator, and we saved her life by giving her CPR we had learned in school. The episode was inspired by a letter sent to the show by a fan. To this day I'm still approached by people who say they saved someone using the CPR they learned on *Punky Brewster.* I love that kids learned important things from what we did on that show. Most of all, I hope that kids learned to be themselves—quirks, curiosity, and all.

I look at my girls now and I'm continually entertained by them. I love it when I see myself in them, and I love it even more when they are totally themselves. I even try not to be too horrified when their little experiments take a wrong turn.

Just the other day Jagger sprayed herself in the face with the bidet. Lovely. And once wasn't quite enough to quench her enthusiasm. So she did it again. She's given dirt a try a few times, too. But whether it's a mouthful of bidet water or a lick of dirt, who am I to judge . . . probably . . .

*　　*　　*

S.P.S.

People are strange . . .

We all want our kids to be happy. And we also want to be good parents. So when our kids are showing their individuality, we can feel conflicted about how to handle it. We want to encourage their uniqueness, but it can be a cruel world out there at times, and we wonder if we should prepare them for that. So what's a good parent to do? I find it helpful to remember how quirky I was as a kid—and realize that I grew up to be a happy and (reasonably) well-adjusted adult. And truthfully, some of my best qualities as a person are directly linked to those quirks that I had as a kid. I don't think I know anyone who didn't have some unique interest or wacky quirks when they were growing up, or, for that matter, as an adult. So how about a little finish-the-sentence to remind us of some of the craziest quirks we had as kids?

When I was a kid, my quirkiest habit was . . .

"Putting cheese slices on my head to make people laugh."

—Alea

"Singing . . . That is all I did was sing."

—Carrie

"Clenching my fists together and placing them against my teeth with excitement."

—Ashley

"Falling down to make people laugh. I still do that on occasion, but unfortunately I don't do it on purpose."

—Nicole A.G.

18

Too Scared to Scream

Question of the day: What is your favorite kid movie of all time?

"The NeverEnding Story."

—Amy

"Wizard of Oz (still is)."

—Annette

"My favorite kid movie was *Annie*. When I was young, I LOVED *Annie*. I even named my black lab Sandy after the dog in the movie."

—Danielle

"Wizard of Oz and *Mary Poppins*. Still to this day and against my boys' better wishes I will kick back and watch both of them when they come on."

—Lisa M.

"My all time favorite film was *Karate Kid*. I remember pestering my parents for ages to let me go to karate school. In the end my dad told me to paint the fence on the back garden the same way as he does in the film as it would be good practice. It wasn't until I had finished that I realized I'd been had."

—Steven

I can so easily remember what it was like to be a kid that sometimes I have to remind myself I'm an adult. And I think that's actually been really good for me as a parent, because I love to have fun with my girls, and I have no problem getting right down on their level and totally enjoying whatever they're doing.

Sometimes, though, as parents, we have to ask ourselves whether the stuff our kids would find fun (and we might find kind of fun, too) is really appropriate for them. Like, maybe my five-year-old isn't ready to watch *Fast Times at Ridgemont High*. Meanwhile, I would have been the little kid watching that movie and loving every second, but my parents were—as you have probably figured out by now—more unconventional. In my total obsession with horror films as a kid, I convinced my dad to take me, my best friend, Tori, and my then-boyfriend Chad to see *Too Scared to Scream* at a seedy old movie theater on Hollywood Boulevard. We were eight years old. Tori and Chad begged to see a different movie, but I was too excited to worry about their fears.

So my dad took us three eight-year-olds to a creepy theater—complete with red seats, red walls, and sticky floors—and then . . . he left us there. I guess he didn't want to see the movie, either. By that point, I don't know if Chad and

Tori were more terrified by the movie or the fact that we were alone in this place without adult supervision, but they were clearly freaking out. Finally, I realized that this outing was becoming a total disaster, and it was time to call my mom. I found a pay phone at the bottom of a long, dark staircase and told her what had happened. I still remember her shouting into the phone, "Your dad WHAT?" Then she raced over to pick us up, and her first stop was my dad's house to find out what on earth he was thinking. I remember him kind of shrugging. He didn't mean to be irresponsible; it's just that to him, this was not a big deal, and the idea of what was appropriate for an eight-year-old kid just didn't really cross his mind. Little did we know then that there were some other issues going on with my dad, and that some of his odd behavior was hinting at an underlying illness. That was something I would only find out later in life. But that's a story for a different chapter.

The truly funny thing about that night is that after my mom rescued Tori, Chad, and me from *Too Scared to Scream*, she took us to the most sappy, G-rated animated kids' movie at Mann's Chinese. Tori, Chad, and I looked at each other in dismay, thinking, *Damn—this is what we get for calling Mom.* Oh well.

I try to strike a balance in these sorts of situations with my kids. But it's hard to figure out that balance, and what's right for one kid might not be right for another. When Poet was four years old, we thought it would be fun to take her to a Hannah Montana concert. I remember seeing Miley Cyrus up on the stage on a motorcycle, and the music was booming and the crowd was hysterical, and I thought, *Hmmm, I guess this is pretty intense for a four-year-old.* Of course, Poet loved it, and everything was fine, but as parents we're faced with all kinds of decisions every day. What music is it okay to listen to? What television shows are okay to watch, and when should they start getting into things like Facebook and Twitter? Is it okay to play video games? What happens when they act out the characters from the games? There are so many questions. Even though I loved *The Amityville Horror* when I wasn't much older than Poet, I would never let her watch it now. If a scary trailer comes on TV and she happens to be watching, I'll rush over and say, "Close your eyes, close your eyes!" And even though I love social media myself, there's plenty of time—later—for Poet and Jagger to get into it.

We can't shelter our kids forever. God knows, no one could have sheltered me—I was too curious to be held back for long. But it's definitely our responsibility as parents to protect our kids' innocence. I hope my girls hold on to the little kids inside of them forever, just the way I have.

And while they are little girls, I want them to savor every minute of it.

*   *   *

S.P.S.

Making the right choices . . .

How do we pick what is right and what is not right for our little ones to be exposed to?

I truly believe that every child is an individual. I don't think we can hold one kid next to another and say that since it is okay for one, then it will be okay for the other. For example, Poet started out loving Scooby-Doo, just like her mother, and Jagger just can't get enough of it. But Poet got a little scared with one episode and now is more cautious about watching it, while Jagger would love to watch a whole marathon if she could.

I think we do the best we can, and the key to making these choices is communication and observing how they absorb what is around them.

Make your choices known . . .

It is also important that the people around you know what you are comfortable with. If you have a babysitter, grandparent, or friend watching your child, then let them know how you feel about what your little ones are exposed to. Make a list of what works for you. Is it okay to watch live-action tween shows, or are you only comfortable with cartoons that are geared toward small children? Also, how do you feel about people being on the phone or responding to texts or e-mails while watching your children? Better to be up-front with them than to get frustrated later.

Reaching out to others . . .

I feel like some of the best insight I get is from other parents. I love turning to my friends, but also to my community through Twitter and Facebook to ask questions. Don't hesitate to call upon your community for advice. Sometimes the best lessons can be taught by strangers. Other times we need the trust of our loved ones. After listening to a flood of insight, take it all with a grain of salt and make the decision that works best for your family. Realize that just like us, every child is his or her own individual. They are not carbon copies, so embrace their uniqueness as you make choices that work best for you.

The girls and me headed to the Hannah Montana concert

19

. . . .

Let's Play the Quiet Game— You Know, the One Where No One Speaks for as Long as Possible . . .

Question of the day: What do you do when you feel like you need a time-out?

"When I need a nice time out I run a nice hot bath, put on some meditation music, and lay in the tub for a long, long time. If it's an overnight time out, I call some girlfriends and make it a Mommy's night out."

—AnnaMae

"That's what the TV is for. Turn on some cartoons and take a break. A half hour of TV won't hurt them."

—Allen

"My hubby works out of town during the week, so it's just me a lot of the time! One big thing that helps me is to put on some music and dance in the living room with my kids. It clears my head to dance and sing and they get to join in! By the end, we're out of breath and usually laughing hysterically."

—Jennifer

"Go for a ride in my car, even if it's to nowhere . . . it helps clear my mind."

—Jill O.F.

"If my husband is home with the kids, I go for a walk, I just soak in my surroundings and breathe, it helps take tension away. If my husband is not home, I wait till my kids are napping or in bed for the night and I read a good book or take a quick bath."

—Whitney

Courtesy of the author

Here's the awesome crew that celebrated Jason's fortieth birthday together. A trip that will never be forgotten.

here I was with a bunch of friends a few weeks ago, float-
ing around in a pool in Mexico, taking in the sun in the
middle of the afternoon, and laughing hysterically while we
read aloud from one of Chelsea Handler's books. No kids,
just adults. It was Jason's birthday, and we'd left the kids
with my mom and taken off for a weekend away.

In the days leading up to our trip, when I'd casually mention to people that Jason and I were going away for his fortieth birthday, I'd see the dramatic head turns of disbelief. They
didn't always say it out loud, but they didn't have to: *You're
leaving the country without your kids? Bad Mommy!* But you
know what? Mommy needed a little time-out.

Working from home is amazing. I love it. I get to do ten
different things at once and still pack lunches, pick up my daughters from preschool, and watch them dance at ballet and sing in
drama class. I can drop work for forty-five minutes and take
them swimming or out for ice cream. And if they're sick, I get to
make them soup and curl up in bed with them. I am truly grateful, and I don't take it for granted that I have this flexibility.

I love having lots of things going on at once. It's the way
my brain works best. Or perhaps I have just convinced myself
of that. Poet said to me the other day, "Mommy, I want to do
everything." And I was like, *Me, too!* But there are definitely
times when I don't feel like I am at my best and I just need to
take a deep breath and have a moment.

My girlfriend Lisa was here with her son the other day,
and I must have seemed a little frazzled, because she looked at
me and said, "Are you having one of your not-so-perfect parenting moments?" It had been a long and full day. The kids
were screaming, running into walls, and finally I rounded up
all the kids, and I said, "Okay, guys, who wants to watch a

movie?" And for about a full hour the kids were mesmerized by the screen and I collapsed on top of the bed. I gave myself a little time-out. It was just what I needed.

As parents we can feel so guilty for taking a little time for ourselves—and sometimes it's other people who make us feel guilty. But I'm convinced that a little grown-up time— whether a night out with your girlfriends, a dinner with your husband, or renting a movie and eating a pint of ice cream by yourself—can make each of us a better parent. It's in those moments that we get to reconnect with our loved ones and often with ourselves.

We came back from Mexico with open arms. The kids had drawn pictures and decorated our house with my mom, and we were so happy to be home. But I was also truly thankful to have had that time with my husband. So next time you need a time-out, put on some music and take a bath and don't feel guilty when you find yourself savoring the moment.

* * *

S.P.S.

. . . .

Take a break even if you can't get away . . .

We all get to the breaking point sometimes, and when I have been less than patient with my girls, I tell myself, *Well, I will try better tomorrow*. Here are some fun ways to give yourself a little break while also entertaining your kids:

- Movies—Plan a trip to the movies. We make it super fun and they love it. It also gives me a chance

to catch my breath when I am exhausted from running after them all day.

- Alternating playdates—Compare notes with some
  friends and make a schedule of playdates so that
  each of you gets a few hours to get away.

- Making art—It's not just for the kids. Get in there
  yourself and make a collage or paint. Don't laugh, but
  I find coloring alongside the girls totally relaxing.

- Exercise—No, not every form of exercise can be
  done with your baby or kids in tow, but some of
  them can: swimming, walks or hikes, even runs.
  And of course there's also biking, roller-skating,
  ice-skating . . . The more you do outdoors, the
  better.

- Trains—If you have a train in your area that is
  kid-friendly, I always find it relaxing. It is fun for
  the kids and for me. I love to sit back and feel the
  breeze while the train chugs away.

- Mani-pedi—Okay, so this may be a girly thing, but
  I know people who take their sons as well. A mani-
  pedi with the kids can be great. It is an indulgence,
  but if you can explain how special it is, they really
  look forward to it and it is fun for both of you.

Date Night . . .

I have found that planning a date night every once in a while
is very important. I know it can be hard, but that time

together can be so great. It is our time to connect. Cherish it. If you don't have a babysitter, then staying up after the kids go to sleep can work, too. Lighting some candles and listening to music is one of my favorite date nights with my husband— simple and special.

If you are struggling with finding "me time" . . .

Getting up before the kids can be the perfect time to relax, work out, or meditate. At least that is what I have been told, but in all honesty I have yet to try this one. My friends like it. My brother wakes up often to go running at five A.M. I can pretty much say wholeheartedly that I don't think I will ever be that person, but sometimes just thinking about it makes me relax and puts me at ease.

20

. . . .

First Comes Love

Question of the day: How has becoming a parent changed your relationship with your spouse?

"I think it has strengthened it. Since we were teens we had a lot against us and on our plates. Not only did we have to prove society wrong but ourselves."

—Carrie

"Dan and I have realized that by having a child we have chosen something larger than the both of us and it is our duty to continually check our priorities. We have learned to let go of the small stuff and love each other in a way our children will hopefully mirror in their own marriages."

—Jill

"It was hard at first, but any kind of change can be challenging. We had to learn to communicate more and we also learned to trust in each other more. Becoming parents has made us more complete."

—Amy L.

"I think being parents has just given us one more area in life to 'balance each other out.' He likes to spend money, I like to save. I freak out when our daughter gets sick, or has a bad day at school, and he's the one who reminds me to slow down and evaluate the situation. Also, we have less alone time. But we make it work :-)"

—Becky

I met the love of my life when I was just eighteen years old. I know, crazy, right? I was busy having fun, being a college student in New York, loving life. And then, there he was, Mr. Right.

I was about seventeen when I wrote my first screenplay, and I'd always had a love for writing, so for college I went to the New School in New York City to study literature and drama. I came home from school for winter break my first year, and I was called in to meet with a production company about a part in a very indie film they were producing. I remember exactly what I was wearing for the meeting—a classy black and silver lacy shirt, black platforms, pleated skirt—and I'd already managed to develop a little New York attitude. Okay, "classy" is probably not the best word to describe my clothing. It was more Manhattan meets Contempo Casuals, but hey, I didn't care. I was feeling totally secure with myself. The director left the room for a minute, and in walked Jason—he was one of the producers on the film. My first thought when I saw Jason? *Well, hello, tall, dark, and handsome.*

Jason on the set of our movie, *1440*. Tall and super handsome.

Anyway, they offered me the part, and I don't know where I got my courage, but I said I'd take the role if they gave me a chance to direct a movie. Jason and the other producers looked at each other and said, "Okay, tell us what your movie is about." So I told them that it was about five kids who thought they had only twenty-four hours to live. Then they kind of gave me a challenge, and said, "Write it in a week, and we'll consider it." So I did. While we were filming the indie movie, I worked every other minute of the day writing that screenplay, and by the end of the week I knocked on my brother Meeno's door with my handwritten manuscript and begged for his help. He sat down at his computer, and while I perched by his side reading the words out loud, he typed the script. We eventually titled it *1440*, for the number of minutes in a single day. The night before I was going back to school, I dropped it on the producers' doorstep and then went back to New York.

A week later, I got the call that they'd make my movie, and then I had to do some serious soul searching. I loved school, and I really loved New York, but when was I ever going to have an opportunity like that again? On top of it, they were going to let Meeno and me direct it together. Finally I decided that I just had to do it. So I dropped out of school, and my brother and I put together an amazing cast— Scott Caan, Danny Masterson, Heather McComb, Jason Lee, Marissa Ribisi, and my really good friend Justin Pierce. Justin had introduced me to a bunch of his skateboarding friends in New York, and I gave a number of them cameos in the movie, too. (In 2000, my incredible friend Justin died tragically, and I still miss him.)

Meeno

Justin Pierce and me on the set of *1440*. So young and full of heart.

We went into pre-production, and a day before filming was scheduled to start, most of the financing fell through. I remember sobbing in Jason's office—I had quit school and thrown my heart and soul into this movie. How could it all fall apart?

Thanks to Jason, it didn't. We found new financing, and making that movie was such an amazing experience—directing with my brother, working with so many of my best friends. It wasn't until a few years later that it really hit me how unreal it was—I was sitting in a movie theater and they were flashing trivia questions on the screen—and there I was, the answer to a trivia question: *Who is the youngest female director in Hollywood history?* It was an incredible feeling.

Over the course of filming, Jason and I became very close friends. Two years after we met, we became a couple. And two years after that, we got married. Did I ever think that I'd be married at age twenty-two? Never. But there wasn't a second that I doubted I was making the right decision. In addition to everything else I loved about Jason, I knew he was the man who would always support my dreams.

I can't believe we've been married for more than twelve years now—although in some ways it's hard to imagine when we weren't married. But I look back and I know that we've both changed and grown in a lot of ways. Of course, the biggest change of all was having our girls. Having babies can throw any couple for a loop, but we keep making it work. I definitely think that a huge part of why it works is that we support each other in everything we do—outside and inside the home.

I discovered quickly that along with being a hands-on parent, it is also important for me to be happy and inspired by what I'm doing in other areas of my life—whether it's writing, designing clothes, my work with the Little Seed, or advocating for Alzheimer's awareness. This all keeps me crazy busy, but it also keeps me totally energized. And luckily Jason's the same way.

I know the classic advice for couples with children is that they should make time to go out on dates. Like that's so easy, right? But we really do try to do it every week. It doesn't always happen. Even if we don't get out alone, though, we always make time to talk to each other. We've made that a huge priority, and we've tried to pass that on to the girls. The same way that Jason and I know that we can talk to each other about anything, we want the girls to know that they can come to us with anything—*anything*. And I really hope we have the kind of open and honest relationship where they always feel safe to do that—no matter what comes up. Before I know it, they're going to be falling in love themselves, or they'll have questions about (oh my God) sex, or smoking, or drinking, or maybe experimenting with drugs. And I want them to know they can come to us with all of them.

I made Poet a collage for her birthday a few months back, but I just never got around to hanging it on the wall. So there it sat, leaning against her wall for weeks and weeks. Finally I made the time to hang it up for her, and I surprised her with it when she came home from school. She was so happy when she saw it. She said, "Oh, Mom, I've been trying to tell you that I've wanted it up for so long." I was so struck by that. I don't know if I wasn't listening well enough before, or if she just had a hard time expressing it clearly, but whatever the reason, I had missed her signals. And then I thought how full my kids' lives are, and I wondered how much gets by us when we aren't paying enough attention to the little things.

So in the same way that Jason and I make sure we set aside time every week for the two of us as a couple, now we've decided to have weekly meetings with the girls so they can talk and be heard, and address all the things they have questions about. We did it with Poet for the first time last week, and it was amazing. She had so much to say! It made us realize that so many of the obstacles we go through in all our relationships—with each other, with our kids—are from miscommunication and not always being heard.

We've always been a family who talks. And now we're a family who talks even more. At dinner the other night, we went around the table to talk about what we were all thankful for. It turned out that Jason and I were thankful for the same exact thing: each other. Two people who fell in love way back in the beginning of time, and now here we were still in love with each other and with our little ones. Through ups and downs, good times and bad, we are on the same team.

Courtesy of the author

Jason and me, always looking out for each other

* * *

S.P.S.

For couples . . .

When our babies are born, we fall head over heels in love with them—so in love, in fact, that it's easy to put their needs above everything else in our lives. But don't forget to take the moments to say "I love you" to your partner and show them how grateful you truly are. We get so crazed that it is easy to forget the little things that mean so much.

For single parents . . .

You are my heroes. Honestly. I often think about how when I'm at my most exhausted, the single parents I know are just as exhausted and have at least twice as much to do. I was raised by a single mom who worked and took amazing care of us, and she gave me such a wonderful childhood. I've never believed that you have to have a two-parent home to raise happy, healthy kids—and don't ever let anyone convince you otherwise.

For all of you . . .

Parents know best how hard it is to balance the needs of work, home, extended family, school, and on and on. When we have babies, it's like we get a membership card to this whole community of parents, and the only requirement is that we give each other a hand now and then. So if your kid is invited to a birthday party and you know your friend could use a break, offer to take her kid to the party with yours. If you know a single parent who's studying for an exam, offer to have her kid come for a sleepover. Take turns dropping your kids off at baseball practice or dance class. Membership has its privileges!

Finally, remember that those family sit-downs can be insightful and fun. Take turns talking about what you are each most grateful for and ask your kids about their week and if they have anything that they really want to talk about. Sometimes the best moments can come from listening.

21

. . . .

The Mack Truck Moment

Question of the day: What has been your Mack Truck Moment?

"Definitely the first day of preschool!"

—Ashley

"My 'baby' just got her learner's permit and turned 16 yesterday—I would say THAT is my Mack Truck Moment. There's no turning back from here! :)"

—Cari

"One would have to be when my little Joseph told me for the first time that he loved me. I would always say it to him before bedtime and he'd smile or hug me, but this one time he said with such confidence, 'I love you too, Mommy!' It was the biggest thing in the world for me!"

—Nicole A.G.

"When the girls start talking about boys. Boyfriend talk. oh no!!!!"

—Nicole P.

HAPPY CHAOS

"When they have a sleep over at a friend's house and don't miss me at all!"

—Ash

Everyone always says to cherish the moment, because they go by in the blink of an eye. They say to take pictures and enjoy all of the precious time you have with your kids because they grow up so fast. What they don't say is that in the midst of all of these special moments, one day you'll feel as though you have been hit by a Mack truck—and that is what happened right before my daughter Poet turned five.

I really feel like I try to live in the moment. I love my kids so very much, and the time we have together fills my heart. But in life we get busy. We get caught up in the day-to-day of living, and sometimes we forget to slow down and just hold on to the snapshot of what is happening all around us. So there I was. Poet was about to turn five and, all of a sudden, one day I felt like a truck came and hit me. The way my baby moved, her hair, the way she spoke . . . I realized, oh my God, she is not a toddler anymore—she is my little girl. Every emotion in the world came over me in that moment and I just wanted to cry.

I couldn't believe it. It was as if in one day she went from being my toddler to transforming into this little lady. Of course, I know this is not something that really happened in one day, but it sure felt like it. And I am sure for each parent that moment happens at different times, but for me it happened on a sunny afternoon in late August—a day I will never forget.

So instead of just telling you to cherish the moment and hold on to it as if there were no tomorrow, I say one day your Mack truck will come, and no matter what, no matter how hard you try, you will not be ready for it. So make sure to have the tissues ready and a lifetime of pictures and memories to back up all of the moments that brought you from the beginning to that magical moment.

Whether it is during the first day of preschool, or when your child is going off to college, we all have this moment. It is what bonds us parents together like glue. The beauty is that our children are always part of us, no matter how old they are. A few weeks after Poet turned five, she came in our room and curled up with us to go to sleep. I looked at her and thought, *Yes, she is still my little baby.* The same week my mother came to see me, and as I gave her a big hug good-bye, I realized, *I am still her baby.* And with that I asked her for one more hug. I needed it just as much as she did.

*   *   *

S.P.S.

. . . .

Hold on to the memories . . .

Keep as many pictures, drawings, letters, and mementos as you can. I love to open the little box where I keep their bracelets from the hospital and their sonograms. It gives me quiet time to reflect and cherish the moment. It is also fun for us to look at pictures together. The girls love it. Once every few weeks, we break out photos, old and new, and talk about them together. I feel like it helps us to hold on to the memories.

22

. . . .

Over-the-Shoulder
Boulder Holder

Question of the day: How do you help your child feel good about their body image?

"We look in the mirror every morning and say I feel good! I look good! And that's what matters and smile real big!"
—Mikala

"I show my children pictures of all different people. I tell them that everyone is different and beautiful, regardless of your body shape, size, how short or tall you are, your skin color, your nationality, your hair etc. I show them how all people have characteristics they might not like, but it makes them unique. 'There is only one you, and you are beautiful!'"
—Sheila

"Well, for only being 3 yrs. old, I just always tell him that he's a handsome little man and he smiles, as though he knows."
—Nicole A.G.

"Neither has had issues with that yet, but I try to tell them not to worry about what others think. We all come in different shapes and sizes, and what matters is that they are happy with their bodies, and they shouldn't try to fit into someone else's mold."

—Dana

Even though I was raised in Hollywood, land of the fit and beautiful, I didn't grow up with many insecurities about my body. I'm sure that was mostly thanks to my mother, but it's also due to the fact that I just love food so much. I can't imagine going through life feeling like I can't have a plate of pasta or dessert.

I look back on pictures of myself, and I definitely went through my chunky phases—right around fifteen, and then again when I went off to college and gained my freshman twenty (yes, *twenty*—and I'm five foot one). I could put away an entire pint of ice cream in my apartment at night, and that's exactly what I looked like when I trotted off the plane in LA for Christmas break that year. But I never remember anyone in my life looking at me sideways when my weight went up or down. And I met my husband and fell in love with him when I had that lovely college weight packed on, so obviously it didn't affect my love life too much.

There was one huge change that took place with my body that I dealt with in a really public way. It's hard enough going through puberty, but it is really fun going through it in front of millions of people, in the public eye. I started developing by the time I was about twelve. Both sides of my family have very busty women, and let's just say I got extra blessed in the boob department. I am sure many remember Punky's first trip to the store to buy a bra and the famous line "Henry, I'm getting boobs." Of course, Punky drew from my own life experiences, so when I was developing, so was she.

By the time I was sixteen, I was overflowing out of a triple-D bra. I loved being voluptuous, but my body just wasn't made for that much cleavage—I had deep indentations in my shoulders from my bra straps, and I had chronic back pain. But the worst part for me was feeling like I couldn't do things that my friends did without even thinking about it—riding a horse, or even wearing a T-shirt or tank top without a bra. At summer camp I remember kids calling me Punky Boobster. Funny, I guess, if it's not you they're talking about. Meanwhile, I remember the awkward feeling of grown men looking at me in a way that wasn't totally appropriate for a teenage girl— and how people's eyes always seemed to go straight to my chest instead of my face.

Physically, I wanted to be a normal teenager. Professionally, I didn't want my build to get in the way of taking on certain roles. So finally, I decided to do something that a number of other actresses my age also did when they faced the same issues—I got a breast

Courtesy of the author

Decked out in my catsuit dress

reduction. It was an incredibly scary decision to make, but one that I was certain would give me a freedom that I desperately needed.

The surgery was intense, and for much of my life I had been nervous when it came to doctors and hospitals. Back when I was eight years old, I had jumped out of a moving car just to avoid getting a tetanus shot, so try to imagine how motivated I must have been to go through with surgery. My friends and family were incredibly supportive, and even when I was in the hospital on intravenous Demerol seeing pink elephants dance around the room, they all trooped in and out of my hospital room to show me their love. I will never forget the support that surrounded me over those following weeks.

I decided to go public with my reduction at that time, and

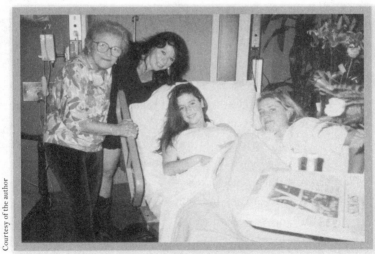

Courtesy of the author

In the hospital right after my surgery with my mom, God-Grandma Jackie, and Krishna. So much love filled my room during those days.

maybe offer some help to other girls going through the same thing. I had lived so much of my life in public up to that point that I felt like I could help others know that they were not alone. I still remember the *People* magazine shoot for their cover story. One of the best parts of the shoot was when my friend Brian Green showed up. We played pool, and afterward he and I went parasailing in Marina del Rey. It was a fantastic day. He was a big part of my life back then, and someone I will always consider a friend who filled my youth with so many happy moments.

And then the *People* issue came out, and there I was filling most of the cover. The rest of the cover featured the massive headline TEENAGE PLASTIC SURGERY. The type was huge, and below it was more: NOSE BOB! BREAST JOB! THINNER THIGHS! It looked like I'd had some kind of full-body makeover at the tender age of sixteen, even though I had not. This was in the days before people really discussed plastic surgery very much, so the idea that I spoke out about it was pretty unusual. People talked about my reduction for years after, perhaps because, unlike others who had more dramatic tales from childhood, this sounded like my darkest hour. It was actually one of my proudest. I am so grateful for the decision I made. No matter what age, it is never too late to feel good and be free. It happened for me at sixteen and for others at sixty. And it was worth it to go public. After that issue came out, I got so many letters from women and girls saying that I had changed their lives. And I still get those responses—just a few weeks ago, a woman came up to me and told me that I'd inspired her to have her own reduction.

I really did feel incredible after I'd had the surgery—like suddenly this thing that had been weighing on me and getting in my way (literally), and had been a huge focus of my energy, wasn't a problem anymore. And it was so great not to be pre-occupied with self-consciousness over my body and how other people might be viewing it.

I'm not saying that I'm completely immune to body inse-curities, but I really don't obsess—not just because I don't want it to spill over onto my girls, but also because it just doesn't make me happy to feel defined by how I look, or to think about it all that much. I don't even have many mirrors in our house (as my friends have often complained when they're looking for someplace to check their hair).

Like many of us, I've been through my phases with exercise, but I'm not fanatical about it. I am so far from being athletic—I mean, Hula-Hooping was one of the closest things I got to sports when I was growing up. But when I started acting on *Sabrina, the Teenage Witch*, I got a little more serious about getting into shape. Then I went through my Pilates phase and that was fun—especially when I did it at Demi's house, with her daugh-ters. She has one of the most amazing bodies ever, so trying to keep up with her was a little tough—but we would laugh the whole time. We would all be lying there with bands around our legs, and I would be in tears while she powered through. I was determined to go for it, or at least not to throw up from exercis-ing too hard. The whole thing was exhausting and exhilarating all at once. My friend Teddy was training us, and he is the work-out king. He would push us harder and harder. It was truly a blast, although my ass killed me during those few months.

When I got pregnant with Poet, I stopped exercising alto-gether and just kind of cocooned. After I gave birth to her, I was never in this crazy rush to get in shape again; I took my time. It's funny, because I'd kind of shrug at the extra pounds and tell myself, *Oh well, I just had a baby.* Then one day I realized I'd been using that line for over a year, and maybe it was actually time to get in shape again. So I did, and then along came Jagger. And now, who in the world has time to get in shape? It's been over two years since Jagger was born, and this is my typical exercise routine:

1. Think to myself, *I'm going to get in shape!*

2. Get on the elliptical for a day.

3. Stop for a week.

4. Repeat.

Maybe I'll really get back in shape once they're both in grade school. Or maybe not. When I think about the time involved, it's hard to imagine it. For now, dancing with my kids to Taylor Swift is my workout. My stomach might be a little soft, but that's nothing a T-shirt can't cover. The important thing is that I'm completely at peace with the skin I'm in, and I want my girls to know that.

*   *   *

S.P.S.

Scratching the surface . . .

It's totally human to compare ourselves to other people. We look at magazines, we watch TV, and we see bodies and lifestyles that are unrealistic. And even if we protect our kids from those images at home, they're eventually going to be exposed to them somewhere else—whether it's at a friend's house, or at school, or on newsstands and billboards. No matter how hard we try, our kids will be exposed to things beyond our control. So what can we do about it? We can try not to fall into that trap ourselves. I think comparing ourselves to other people is one of the worst things we can do for own self-esteem, and for our kids' self-image as well.

Leading by example . . .

I never try to censor what my kids eat, but we do things in moderation. We indulge in pizza, but we eat it with salad, or sometimes we even eat salad pizza. We truly make it fun, and I have found that the joy of eating is so very important to them and how they deal with food.

What about the things that make our children unique?

Even my five-year-old has questions about her body. It starts so early. Both of my kids are very tall for their age. So funny, considering how little I am. We talk about it, and I tell them how lucky they are. When we go to the amusement park, we make it special that Poet is tall enough to go on the rides. Instead of making her feel like an outsider because of her height, we try to embrace it and encourage her to feel great about it. When our little ones go through a hard time growing up and with puberty, the best thing I can say is to try to listen to them and to be there. I think trust is incredibly important, and how we deal with our own self-image is sure to come up. I will try to pass on my own experiences to my kids while encouraging them to feel good about themselves.

What happens when that special day comes?

I will never forget the day I started my period. I was wearing a silk robe with butterflies and I couldn't believe it. I went and told my mom and she turned it into a celebration, full of toasts and everything. Now, I'm not saying to break out the champagne and embarrass your child, but maybe giving them something special, a gift as their entry into womanhood, might be nice. Something between the two of you that is shared can be a great way to kick off going through puberty. I think it also creates a closeness to be remembered.

23

Jake Ryan, Where Are You?

Question of the day: Who was your favorite eighties character of all time?

"Easy—Wonder Woman! She kicked butt in a man's world and looked great the entire time!"

—Jill H.

"Punky Brewster. And I'm not just saying it because she was you. She was an inspiration to me. She was my age, and not afraid to be herself. I was kinda shy as a kid and didn't really go out of my way to be noticed. Punky helped me come out of my shell :-)"

—Becky

"It's a toss up between Buddy from *Charles in Charge* and Troy Garland from *Out of This World*. There's something that still makes me chuckle every time I think of Evie talking to her alien dad with a crystal cube."

—Ashley

Where do I begin to speak about my love for this man? I can't remember exactly when I first fell in love with Jake, but it was a love affair that would last for a lifetime, or at least until I found my own Jake. Something about his smile and charm just melted my heart, along with every other girl in America. And that red car—oh, how I loved that moment when he pulls up to the church—I must have put myself into Molly Ringwald's shoes a thousand times. Then there is the song. The song that has been a theme throughout my life. With the cake between them as he tells her to make a wish and she tells him that it already came true. Yummy, sweet, lovable Jake. Yes, I tried to find him over the years and yes, along with every other girl who has Googled Jake Ryan, or the actor who played him, I know he became a woodworker or something, but I couldn't find out much more than that. Perhaps the tremendous number of infatuated women was just too much for him to handle, but let's not think of that.

Let's just pretend, as I do, that he was real. Just as real as any other great figure who has lived throughout time. Jake is right up there for me. John Hughes movies were my favorite, and even on the night before my wedding, I stayed up watching *Sixteen Candles* with Tori and then again in the morning. I had to explain to Jake as he came onto the screen that even though we had a love affair, my heart now belonged to someone else—but that no matter what, I would always carry a special place for him.

I was always honest with my husband about Jake. I never hid it from him, and he has come to embrace Jake over the years. He even made a film for my birthday with Jake in it as an honor to what could have been. When my husband really wants to warm me up, he will play me the cake song. Yes, it's true, although I'm sure he is not thrilled that I am sharing this with the world. But you see, that is one of the things I love so very much about Jason. He accepts me one hundred percent for who I am and even inspires me to hold on to that piece of make-believe that I have carried for so long. Over the years I have met a lot of guys. There were my guy friends who were more than friends but not officially boyfriends; there was my phase of having crushes every other week, and my dating stages. But my first real boyfriend became the love of my life. I married him at twenty-two, and two children and over twelve years later, I am still crazy about him. I found my Jake.

* * *

S.P.S.

A little sentence to finish . . .

My favorite memory from the eighties was . . .

"The Duran Duran haircut"

—Mikala

"Sleepovers with my friends. We would blast Madonna and sing into hairbrushes!"

—Sheila

"When Tom Cruise slid across the silver screen in a button down shirt and his tighty whities in the movie *Risky Business*! Oh how my heart throbbed and still skips a beat for that character. Love Tom!"

—Dawn

"A mini-concert that I, my brother and cousin threw for my Grandma in the backyard. I was wearing my gray parachute pants, with purple jelly shoes, Duran Duran t-shirt and headband on. A close runner-up favorite 80's memory would have to be buying my first tape and it was Michael Jackson's *Thriller* album. Loved it!"

—Nicole A.G.

What happens when that first heartbreak comes along?

What will I do when one of my girls comes home with her first heartbreak? Grab a pint of ice cream, curl up together for a John Hughes marathon, and dream about Jake. . . .

24

. . . .

Girl Time

Question of the day: What is your favorite thing to do with your friends?

"Get our kids together and take them all on a mystery trip usually to a water park beach or someplace else fun to go that everyone enjoys."

—Amelia

"Daydream about weekends away without kids and husbands while the kids wrestle around us."

—Amy

"Sit and talk—about everything, about nothing. Just to sit and be myself—good or bad."

—Jessica

"Go places and talk—hear live music together. Share a movie."

—Kathryn

Even though I'm officially an adult, one thing about being a kid that I never want to let go of is the friendships. Remember those friendships from when you were little? Remember all your friend-crushes as you got older, and how those friendships totally defined who you were at any given moment? And have you ever laughed harder than when you were with a few of your best friends?

Now that I'm a wife and mother, of course my husband and my kids are the most important relationships in my life. But I still need my girlfriends. I need them to support me when I'm down, be happy for me when something goes right, or just let me be that silly girl that I always keep inside.

I'm incredibly lucky that I get to work with my best friend, Tori. But even though we spend a lot of time together, we still have to make sure that we carve out time that isn't all about work or the kids. During the holidays she comes and sleeps over. We get up early in the morning, go to the flower market, and then cook all day long together. Moments standing beside her in the kitchen, making mashed potatoes and cooking for our family feast, are some of my favorite memories.

One of my oldest girlfriends is Melissa Joan Hart. We met during casting for Ron Howard's show *Little Shots* when we were both about seven years old. Fast-forward a couple decades, and we were both pregnant with our first babies at the same time. We truly became close friends when we were in our early twenties. We would spend late nights talking, while Jason gave her advice about guys. When she was cast in a play in New York, I came along and we shared an apartment for a month, having a total blast and going out to sing karaoke at night. I was already married to Jason at this point. But he knew I needed some girl time—or a whole month of girl time. She was starring then in

Sabrina, the Teenage Witch and soon I was cast to play her college roommate, Roxie King. I remember during filming we would lie on the floor of her trailer and we'd talk about *everything* for hours upon hours. I love that now as moms we still try to carve out time together, even if it is just for a half-hour frozen yogurt run.

Lisa Rowe

Here I am with my good friend, Melissa Joan Hart

Somewhere inside of us, we will always be the seven-year-old girls we were when we first met. That never goes away.

Of course, it's a lot harder to see our friends when we've got a family—especially if not all of our friends have kids. When we have so much to do at home, it can be incredibly hard to make the time for our friends, especially since that means also making time for ourselves, which so many parents find difficult. It's really easy to let those relationships get put to the side while we focus on what's in front of us. But whether you only have long enough for a quick coffee with a friend during the workday or a side-by-side pedicure, or you have the luxury of a real girls' night out, you have to make the time. Otherwise, one of these days your kids will be off having their own social lives and you'll realize, hey, wait a second—what happened to *my* social life?

Every few months my friends Lisa, Ariana, Rebecca, and I all manage to get away for a lunch, just us girls. They're hard to arrange, but so worth it—not only for us, but for our kids, too. We talk about everything, and it feels so good to know that someone is listening and understands what the other is going through. I think it's really important for my girls to see that I work hard on my friendships and that those relationships are something to aspire to. And when they're having a conflict with a friend (which seems to happen more and more as the girls get older), I want them to know how important it is to work it out. You don't just get frustrated and walk away. And if they're as lucky as I have been, the same girls they're tied at the hip with now will be the first people they call at every turn of the road for the rest of their lives.

Courtesy of the author's friends

Me, Rebecca, Arianna, and Lisa at one of our fun lunch dates

* * *

S.P.S.

The importance of friendships . . .

I will never forget all of the friendships that touched my life as a kid. My best friend, Tori, and I have memories of traveling the world together. We went everywhere, from New York and Nashville to Puerto Rico and the Caribbean. And we would always go on some kind of adventure. My mom would take us on carriage rides in Central Park. We would climb rocks and think we were near death on the highest points in the Virgin Islands. We had endless sleepovers, laughter, tears, and more laughter. I want my kids to grow up with the understanding of how much our circle of friends means in our lives. I am truly grateful that I can look at the people around me and so many of their faces flash back to childhood. My good friend Sarah Gilbert and I grew up together since we were about ten. We spent holidays and many fun nights together throughout our youth. I love that when I see her face, I see the same cool girl who wore a blue and purple tie-dyed shirt at our first sleepover. Just this Christmas Eve, as I looked around at Sarah with her beautiful kids; Tori cooking up a storm; Danny Masterson with his whole family; Chrissy, my summer camp friend who was wise beyond her years; and all

Sondra Peluce

Me and Tori: kids having fun in the sun in the Caribbean

of the other faces that I spent my youth and adulthood with, I thought about just how blessed I am. There is the family we are born into and the family we choose, and here were both, together. . . . Now, pick up the phone and call a friend you haven't talked to for a while, and I'm going to do the same. :)

Remember to talk about things other than our kids . . . no matter how hard it is . . .

How many times has this happened to you: You get together with your friends for the first time in ages, and you spend the whole time talking about your kids. That's great sometimes, but it's really healthy (and very much appreciated by your friends who don't have kids) to remember all those interesting subjects you used to talk about before you were a parent. So next time you're with your friends for an adults-only gathering, try to open up the conversation to other topics as well. Better yet, if you have a ladies' night together, you could make a drinking game out of it. Whoever talks about her kid first has to drink. Everyone will probably wind up very intoxicated—just kidding, but not really.

Carving out time . . .

That precious time with our friends is so important, and we need to remind ourselves to take it. Trading off with your partner or friends is a great way to make a little girl time. Tell your friend, family member, or partner that you would love to trade a night out for a night out. Support each other. A little space to remember the individuals we were before we had kids is refreshing for all of us.

25

· · · · · · · · · · · · · ·

The Much-Needed
Family Vacation

Question of the day: What's your favorite family vacation memory?

> "A very long road trip to California from Colorado. Swimming in hotel pools with my dad, and laughing the whole time at his jokes." —Cari

> "It was when my family and I went to a ranch resort in Arizona. My children were riding the horses and the smiles on their faces were just priceless!"
>
> —Ashley

> "Meeting Mickey and Minnie Mouse!"
>
> —Dana

> "Visiting Grandpa and swimming with him in the pool. It was such a moment! My son Joseph loves the water! It's the simple things in life that matter the most."
>
> —Nicole A.G.

Courtesy of the author

Here we are on our family vacation in Mexico

We get so busy in our everyday lives that we often forget to find the balance.

Between school drop-offs and work, we get busier and busier, and before we know it, months have gotten away from us. Other than family dinners, moments during the weekend, and limited time between work projects, we sometimes forget to take the time with our family to really nurture each other and ourselves.

Something incredible happened to me this past holiday season—something that, had I not experienced it myself, I may have overlooked completely. The experience has opened my eyes in a whole new way.

In the midst of our family's busy life, it became more and more clear to me that my kids were getting bigger faster than I could catch my breath. They were breaking out of the cocoons that once nurtured them, and becoming more and more their own people.

I couldn't believe it, and yet I couldn't stop it, either. My two-year-old was getting bigger by the second and my five-year-old seemed to be turning fifteen.

I was struggling. I felt more lost as a parent than ever before. I started questioning every move I made up until that point. Had I done something wrong? Was it okay that on a few occasions I had let them watch *Hannah Montana* or music videos? They love pop music, but were they being too exposed to things they shouldn't be? Was I pushing them to grow up too fast? I immediately started monitoring them more. We started doing more reading, playing, and cooking together— anything to keep them kids for as long as possible.

We had regular heart-to-hearts as a family and an open line of communication, but I still felt they needed more from us. At one breaking point I found myself in the bookstore looking for books that could give me insight. Here I stood with a thousand pregnancy, newborn, and toddler books, but I wondered about the next steps. There was a void on the bookshelves, and the message seemed to be "If you haven't figured it out by now, you are screwed." I came home and wondered what to do next. How do I become the best parent I can be to my children?

Then something amazing happened that truly shifted things. It was over the holidays and we decided to try to shut everything else down and just be with the kids. On Christmas morning we opened presents, and then Jason handed me an envelope and there it was . . . Inside were two passports that he had gotten for our daughters, and a homemade gift certificate for a trip to Mexico. I couldn't believe my eyes. We were leaving in less than a week. I was thrilled! And then the anxiety set in. How would I meet my work deadline? What about the girls' school, etc? Then I realized that I needed to just let go.

So a week later we began our journey together, just us and the girls, and immediately I realized that this was exactly what our children needed—and what Jason and I needed. It was time for us to be a family—no work, no babysitters, no distractions from each other. We played in the pool, read books, drew, and ate together. We walked and danced. We took each other in and did it with open arms. I took the time to ask the girls regularly what they needed, not just in terms of the day, but in life. We cuddled, we laughed, and we shared. When a meltdown would arise, I would find myself handling it with a calm that does not come to me quite as easily when we are in the throes of everyday life. I am aware that not everyone has the luxury to take a family vacation like this. But whether it is a camping trip for a few nights, a campout in the living room, or a hike in the woods, we can carve out that time to just be together. Roasting s'mores, telling stories, playing ball, swimming, and laughing hard. Making that time for our kids to know that their voices will be heard, and that what they have to say really matters, will make all of the difference in the world to their evolution as people. I guarantee it is those memories they hold on to. Some of my greatest memories growing up were when my mom would take my big brother and me on a trip. She would save up all year to take us someplace special, and those moments are some of the closest to my heart.

So take that family vacation. Everything else can wait. Know that it is the best investment for our little ones. No matter how short or long your trip, the most important thing is that when you are with them, you are present, and that it is not ten or twenty percent of Mom or Dad that your kids get, but the whole package.

And after the kids go to sleep, it is the perfect time to have some alone moments as grown-ups. You can snuggle up, read to each other, or watch a movie, and take time to share and reflect on the life you are building together. It gives you strength for the love you share and respect for the parents you are.

* * *

S.P.S.

Planning a family vacation . . .

Planning a family vacation can be fun, but it can also be stressful, so try to do it together. What is something that all of you can enjoy? Another fun idea is to take turns planning it. Family vacations don't need to break the bank. A super-fun family vacation can be a "staycation." Decorate your living room like Hawaii or with a Japanese theme. You can hang pictures and put up a tent in the center of the room draped with different fabrics. You can surprise your little ones and say, "We are going to Japan (or Hawaii) for a few days," and read stories inspired by the culture, or cook foods that you would eat in that place. Some of the best family vacations can happen right in the comfort of our own homes. It is the point of making it special and unique that they will remember, not the cost or extravagance of it. Some of my favorite family vacations were when my mom would lay out some blankets on the small balcony of our little apartment and we would sleep under the stars.

26

Embarrassing Moments

Question of the day: What is your most embarrassing
moment ever?

"Falling down the stairs in high school while the guy I
liked was right there, downstairs, with his friends and saw
me landing on my butt!"

—Amelie

"As a klutz with a recurring case of foot-in-mouth-disease
there are a lot, but probably the worst was in the 6th grade
(right when girls start caring a lot what people think about
them) my family went to Jamaica and I got corn rows. My
mom asked me the night before I went back to school, to
let her take them out, but I was tired and went to bed.
Then in the morning I realized I didn't want to go to
school with them so I asked her to take them out and she
said no, that she would do them that night (she was busy
getting 4 kids off to school). So, I went into the bathroom
and did it myself and came out with a GIANT 70s afro and

asked to take a shower to flatten it. She said she wouldn't let me be late because I had made a bad choice and sent me like that, ensuring months of torture and teasing!"

—Kelly F.

"7th grade. Everyone has that one teacher that's just cute. Mine was gorgeous, just graduated college, and had to wear a tie because he was getting confused with high school guys. One day we were messing around in our 'free time' in class. I was doodling . . . hearts and cupid and love stuff. He walked by my desk to see his name in a heart with mine. He bent down and said he was taken. My face turned bright red."

—AnaLiesa

"I'm still embarrassed about this. I grew up dirt poor. I was 12 years old, and finally able to wear a real bra. It was a hand me down bra though from my mother's friend. My mom put the bra in the dryer so it melted the plastic part that snaps. I only had one bra, and that was it. So, all my mom could find was a HUGE safety pin that was rusted. One day at school it was raining outside so we had to go into the gym to wait for the bell. I was sitting slumped over, and as a guy was walking by I hear 'Ouch! Man something is coming out from her back, and it cut me.' I was mortified. I walked real fast to the bathroom to see what had happened. The safety pin had come undone, and was sticking out of my shirt. I fixed it, and when I got out of the bathroom my friend was asking what was wrong. I just ignored her and went to class. And yes I had to wear that bra the next day, and the rest of the school year."

—Shelley

'm really, really used to embarrassing myself. In fact, I'm so used to it that most of the time I just laugh when it happens.

Probably one of my most truly embarrassing childhood moments happened when I was eight years old and I met Muhammad Ali. He was being honored at a big celebration in Century City, and I was beyond excited. My dad was a boxer (a four-time Golden Gloves champion), so I'd grown up loving boxing and totally loving Ali. And there he was, in a beautiful white tuxedo, surrounded by fans. I was waiting to meet him, in complete awe, when someone from *Entertainment Tonight* decided it would be a great moment to film The Greatest holding Punky Brewster. Unfortunately, I was holding a Cherry Coke at the time, and when the overenthusiastic producer lifted me in the air to Ali, my drink went flying all over his face and his gorgeous white tuxedo. I was horrified. Beyond horrified. I swear the room went silent. Then, with a twinkle in his eye, Ali looked at me and said, "Did youuuuu do this to meeeeeeee?" before breaking into laughter.

Parents are always swapping stories about the embarrassing things their kids do and say. And yeah, we've had our share. Like the time we went to a big party and Poet made friends with the daughter of a famously gap-toothed rocker. Poet looked up at him and said, "You are missing your tooth?" The rocker looked kind of shocked and he said, "Uh, what did you say?" I immediately cut in and said, "Oh, she just said she likes your tattoos!" Unfortunately he had perfectly good hearing, and he knowingly replied, "No, she didn't. She said that I am missing my tooth." He smiled and I smiled back. Whoops.

To be honest, I'm more likely to embarrass my kids than

the other way around. Luckily, they didn't get to see my per-
formance at Walt Disney Concert Hall. A few years ago my
husband took me there to see the Los Angeles Philharmonic.
As much as I love classical music, I had never been to the
symphony before, so I was beyond excited. The music was so
beautiful, but every time it stopped, I would clap and cheer. I
couldn't figure out why no one else was clapping. I was getting downright upset about it—here were these incredible
musicians playing their hearts out for us, and the audience
was too blasé to show their appreciation. So I decided to stand
up and clap over and over again! Finally my husband explained
to me that you don't applaud between movements at sympho-
nies. I sat back down as everyone stared at me in disbelief.

And then there are all the wardrobe malfunctions I've had
in my life. In Hollywood, I'm constantly missing the mark
when it comes to what to wear. I had a meeting a few weeks
ago, and it was really hot. Not to brag, but I rarely sweat.
(Believe me, I have other issues, but that's not one of them.)
But that day, I don't know if I was nervous, or if it was the silk
blouse I was wearing, but my pits turned into round, wet
moons of perspiration. Somehow I didn't notice my expanding
pit stains while I was waving my arms around in the meeting.
Then I went to the bathroom and caught a glimpse in the mirror. One look at myself, and I wanted to lock the door and
never come out. I ripped my blouse off and tried waving it
around to dry it out, but it was no use, and for the rest of the
meeting I kept my arms glued to my sides.

A super-hip and cool friend of mine had a birthday party
for her daughter the other day, and the girls and I were invited.
I didn't have a whole lot of time to figure out what I was

wearing, but I managed to pull something together and thought I looked fine . . . until I got to the party and stood next to the truly fashionista moms. Meanwhile, I looked like I was headed to the playground. A friend of mine finally leaned over to me and said, "Soleil, is your sweater *supposed* to be inside out?" Uh, no.

For Halloween, we went to a local pumpkin patch, and apparently I was the only person in the neighborhood who didn't know that this was *the* Hollywood see-and-be-seen pumpkin patch. It was a huge scene when we got there—video camera crews, photographers, and celebrities in cute outfits posing with their kids and their pumpkins. Meanwhile I was braless, wearing a North Face sweater, baggy jeans, and a beanie. I didn't want to see and be seen. I just wanted a pumpkin!

Now that Poet's getting older, she doesn't hesitate to let me know when I'm embarrassing her. There was a Mommy & Me ballet class at her dance school this week, and although my husband has always told me that I have two left feet, I couldn't wait to go. When we got there, all the little girls were paired off with their moms, but Poet refused to dance with me. She actually told me that she was too embarrassed. Ouch. So Poet danced with her friend, and I danced with her friend's grandmother. Then I thought, well, I might as well go for it, right? You would have thought I was on *Dancing with the Stars*, the way I threw myself into that class. Let's just say that it wasn't pretty.

But there's hope for me yet. After that class, I signed up for dance classes with Poet's teacher. I figure, if she can teach five-year-olds to dance, then she can teach me to dance. And I am really excited, even though I'm sure there will be plenty of embarrassing moments. I can just imagine all of the moms pulling up to a studio of preschoolers and seeing me there in my ballet clothes tripping over myself as I demi-plié. They are welcome to laugh all they want, and I will be doing the same, because no one loves laughing at herself as much as I do.

Suzi Haydon

Jagger and me dressed up in eighties clothes. We love to have eighties dance parties, and Mama loves to embarrass herself.

* * *

S.P.S.

How to deal with those eye rolls . . .

I knew that eventually my sweet babies would grow up and roll their eyes at me over something. But I had no idea it would happen so soon! The important thing is not to take it personally and not to make too big a deal out of it. Children go through this at different ages. One week your child is happy for you to walk them to school hand in hand, and the very next day they drop your hand at the entrance. It can be really emotional for a mom or dad because it feels like the first step on a path of letting go. And in a way, it is. But it's important to remember that even as our kids are maturing, they still need us. So when your child is suddenly horrified that you hugged them in front of their friends, or waved to everyone on the playground, take a deep breath and remember that it is not about you. Just yesterday, I walked into Poet's school to pick her up in overalls and a hat. She shouted in horror in front of her classroom filled with kids: "Mom, what are you wearing?" She then told me that I can't dress like a cowboy/cowgirl. Well, this cowboy/cowgirl is proud—proud that I can let go and laugh at myself. And isn't that one of the best things we can teach our kids, how to laugh at ourselves?

A little sentence to finish . . .

My parents really embarrassed me as a kid when they . . .

"Used to tease me in front of my friends about which heart throb poster or picture was sticky-tacked on my bedroom door that week."

—Ashley

"Wanted to come into my friends' houses when they dropped me off."

—Sheila

"Never failed . . . As a teen, no matter when or where, which friend I had over, they always managed to have the urge to pop out their false teeth in front of my friends. One day on a mall trip, my mom decided to embarrass me on the escalator. She was talking to my friend right before she stepped on and then popped out the teeth. They flew out of her mouth and clattered down the escalator steps. I think that cured her."

—Annette

"Would tell corny jokes to my friends."

—Dana

"Would run late picking up my carpool. Or when my dad let my nickname slip in that very carpool (Dinky) and that is what everyone called me from that day on."

—Jeannette M.

"Mom would sing very loudly in the car, as she was taking me & some friends to the movies. Funny thing is all my friends thought that I had the coolest Mom. I secretly did, too. :o)"

—Nicole A.G.

27

· · · · · · · · · · · · ·

Sticks and Stones

Question of the day: How do you help your kids when they have hurt feelings?

"I listen to them. I ask them what's wrong and try to help them feel better. I often offer a compromise so that everyone is happy. Usually this is the best solution and one that I feel teaches them about life in a deeper way that they may not fully understand just yet."

—Jeannette C.

"Console them and try to explain the situation, whether it's concerning a mean kid or life giving them lemons. I also tell them it's ok to feel that way, and encourage them to share their feelings with me, no matter what those feelings are."

—Dana

"I always talk to my kids about why they are sad or mad. I don't always get answers. It lets them know I am there.

I might not always agree with what they say but they will always be supported."

—Luna

"You can't! That's the real deal. Don't sugar coat it, it's a learning process. It's life. But we can be there for them to console them to let them know we care. If it's us that hurt their feelings, then own up, explain & apologize! We're all human!"

—Chaz

Think of all the little fights you got into with your friends in school over the years. One day you were the best of friends, and the next day your best friend announced that she was besties with someone else. It was tragic.

Now take all that emotion and multiply it ten times over, and that gives you a sense of what it was like on the set of *Punky Brewster.* There were only a few of us kids on the set day in and day out, and we worked together, went to school together, played together. We were like friends and siblings combined. It was *intense* at times. Plus, we were all actors. Oh, the drama! For the most part we got along great, but we did have our moments.

One day when we were all seven or eight years old, Ami did something to upset me, and that night I had a sleepover at Cherie's house. I drew a picture of Ami—not flattering—and I think I may even have written her name on it. The next day, the picture fell out of my notebook at school, and Ami saw it. She burst into tears, and then I burst into tears.

I don't think I have ever felt so totally ashamed in my life. I was not that person—the mean girl who likes making other girls feel bad about themselves. But in that moment suddenly I thought, *Oh my God, I* am *mean! I'm a mean, awful person!* Sobbing, I ran out of the classroom, across the soundstage, across the lot, down halls, and I just ran and ran and ran.

Finally I found a little office down a long hallway and I crawled underneath a table to wallow in my misery. After a while I heard footsteps enter the room. Then the face of one of the assistant directors appeared in front of me, peeking below the table. There was a crackle of his walkie-talkie, and I heard him say, "We found her. She's in Johnny Carson's office."

It turns out that the entire Punky crew was out trying to find me while I was hiding in the King of Late Night's private office. Now I felt horrible and embarrassed, and I walked back to the set full of apologies. And then of course we were all friends again—until the next time one of us got mad at one or more of the others. That's life—on and off of a television set.

I look at my girls now, and I want to protect them from every possible insult they could ever absorb from the world— as if that's possible. I know that I'm supposed to let them learn to stand up for themselves and work things out with their friends—but it's so hard sometimes, especially when their feelings are hurt. That just breaks your heart.

Poet *loves* ballet, and she's been taking it for over a year, so she was incredibly excited to start ballet camp this summer. We went the first day, and she liked it just fine, but then the next day she seemed really nervous to go back. Jagger and I went with her to class just as we'd done the day before, and as we were getting in, I remembered that I hadn't taken Poet to the bathroom. A not-yet-five-year-old definitely needs to go the bathroom before jumping around in a leotard. So I whispered to her—obviously not quietly enough—"Hey Poet, let's go to the bathroom." Suddenly a commotion went up around the room, and one of the older girls said, "Eeeeew, you have to go to the bathroom. Yuck!" Then all the other girls picked up the chorus. Poet was mortified, and I was horrified. Then I got totally defensive. "She's helping me with her little sister!" I said. As if I had anything to justify to a bunch of little girls. It was like I was five years old myself. Oh, how quickly those memories of childhood tragedies come flooding back.

When we got into the bathroom, Poet said, "I don't want to stay, Mommy." I tried to make her feel better and not take it so personally—I said, "Honey, it's okay, sometimes people in life say things they don't mean . . . not because they don't like you, though!" Then I told her that in life we'll have challenges, not everyone will be nice all the time, but in your heart know that you're a really good person, and that's why it's important to be kind to others. Meanwhile, she was looking at me with her sad eyes, and everything I said sounded like an excuse. It was killing me, and all the while I was trying not to say what I was really thinking: *Those girls were being mean!*

So we went home, and Poet was still inconsolable. I called Jason to tell him about the class, and how I had run out of things to say to Poet. He said, "Let me talk to her."

This became one of those times when I fell in love with my husband all over again. Poet listened intently, then she said, "Okay, Daddy," and she handed me the phone. Then she danced away like nothing had happened.

I said to Jason, "What did you say to her?" Seriously, it was like a magic transformation had just taken place.

This is what he told me he said to her: Some days our friends don't feel as loved as they should, so they spread that hurt around. We're lucky we have a family that loves each other and is kind to each other. Sometimes we hurt each other's feelings, too, but we apologize and then we come back around.

Wow. It was simple, not defensive, not angry. Just clear, and calm, and loving. And I could tell just by looking at Poet's face that she got it.

Of course I know that she'll get her feelings hurt again. But I also know that (eventually) she'll be okay, because she'll remember what her daddy said. And so will I.

* * *

S.P.S.

Way back when . . .

Close your eyes. Now remember back to when you were seven or eight years old. Who was your best, best friend? Do you have that person's name and face in your head? Okay, now relish the memories of all of the rights and wrongs you did together and how that helped make you who you are today. When you fought with your friends, did your parents get in the middle, or did you resolve it yourself? I think we can learn so much from the children that we were and the parents that we have become.

Teaching compassion . . .

Just as awful as it is to see our child hurt by another child, it can be downright horrifying when we see or hear that our child has hurt another child. I think it is really important to talk to our kids about kindness and compassion and also to allow them to teach us as well. Just the other day Poet said to me that I was being bossy to others. At first I was horrified but then I realized that she was trying to open my eyes to something that I obviously couldn't see. I leaned down to her eye level and said that it is not nice to be bossy toward others and that I don't want to be that way. I then thanked her for helping me see it. I really believe that when kids feel as though they are a part of your learning experience, they feel more passionate in their own growth.

Picking up on the little things around them . . .

A few months ago my girls went through a phase of acting a little edgy. I couldn't figure it out, the eye rolls and flipping of the hair. I kept thinking to myself, *What in the world is going on?* They had a favorite movie that they loved watching. Every few days, I would let them indulge in it. One day as I was sitting with them watching it, I noticed one of the characters acting out. In that moment I realized they were copying the character. I then sat down with them and explained that the girl on-screen was playing someone who is not nice and that she is a character and we don't want to copy what she does. They really listened to what I said and took it to heart. Now if a character in a movie is acting out, Poet will say, "Don't worry, Mommy. I won't act like that." This can happen with friends, commercials, and just observation of the people and world around us. They are human sponges, so I always try to pay attention to what is going on in their environment and have a deeper understanding so that I can help guide them through it.

So next time you're at the dinner table, or you're watching a television show, and you're discussing situations where people hurt the feelings of others, talk it through. I believe communication is the best recipe for connecting with our little ones.

28

· · · · · · · · · · · · · ·

The Dash Between

Question of the day: How do you talk to your kids about difficult subjects?

"I talk to them like people. I don't break it down in baby language—if they don't understand, they ask for explanations."

—Cari

"Openly and honestly. I want my girls to be able to come to me with any problem, no matter what it is. I try to keep it simple, though, so it's easier to process. Sometimes that approach doesn't work out too well, though. When explaining to my 5 year old what her daddy does (he's in the army), I told her 'He is protecting people from bad guys.' Her response was 'Like zombies?'"

—Dana

"I have found that telling the truth to my daughter has her coming back to me time after time to 'get the truth.' No matter how tough the issue, I stick to the facts. I also try to tell her what I did at her age in that situation & what I would have done differently & the outcomes that are possible."

—Kimberly

Lately it's really hit me how fleeting everything is. The time we have on this earth, the time we have with our babies, and our families, and our dear friends—it's all incredibly short, and so precious.

Bryten Goss was one of my best friends since kindergarten. As an adult he became a highly regarded artist. Then, at age thirty, he took a trip to Mexico for an art project, and when he came home, a virus attacked his heart. He died a few weeks later. It was a horrible shock to all of us who loved him. His amazing mother, Rose Goss, would always say, "There's the time you're born, the time you die, and the dash in between. The important thing is what you do with that dash." This is such a beautiful sentiment that I've never forgotten it.

Bryten's life was way too short, but

Meeno

Bryten and me at one of his art showings

what he did with that dash he spent with us was incredible. He traveled the world and painted places that drew you into his world so completely. You would look at his artwork and it was as if he had lived a thousand lives before because he was that deep and soulful.

I've been blessed to know so many wonderful people who have done inspiring things with their dash on this earth. And they have made my world so much more colorful, rich, and meaningful.

My godfather, Joseph, was the patriarch of our family, and he and I were incredibly close. He was a truly amazing director, and he always encouraged me in all of my creative pursuits. When I wrote my first screenplay, a gangster story called *Blood and Brotherhood*, he was the first person I sent it to. He was there when I was born, and he walked me down the aisle when Jason and I got married. Joseph was there for every important milestone in my life.

Not too long before Poet was born, we found out that Joseph had cancer. No one wanted to hold on to life more than Joseph did, and he pursued every treatment imaginable. He didn't miss a single big event in my life, even when he was terribly sick—he and my amazing godmother, Patricia, traveled all the way from Hawaii for my baby shower, and they stayed for Poet's birth. One of my most treasured memories is when Joseph held Poet in the hospital.

Before Joseph's health really started to fail, he had gone to Bhutan to make a documentary on solar power. It was his dying wish to finish the movie, so we made a bedroom for him in our house in Los Angeles, and we set up ramps so we could wheel him into the house. In our dining room, we installed a television, and there Joseph and his editor finished the movie.

While he stayed with us, Joseph and I had long conversations every evening, and I'm still so grateful for that intense, beautiful time with him. This was back when Poet was just a baby, and she'd cry at night. I remember I'd come down in the morning and ask Joseph if Poet had kept him awake. He'd smile and say, "It just makes me realize I'm still alive." One of the last days he was with us in LA, even though he was weak with pain, he insisted on stopping to get Poet the biggest Halloween pumpkins you've ever seen. And that was just the nature of who he was. He was going to live life to the fullest as long as he could.

Soon it became clear that he only had a few months to live, and he and Patricia wanted to go back to Hawaii for his final weeks. I talked to him constantly over the next few months, and then the first week of January I spoke to him and he said, "Get out here soon." I asked him to promise that he'd wait for me, and he did. But again he said, "Just get here soon."

I left the next day with Poet and Tori. By the time we got to Hawaii, we were exhausted, and we were juggling Poet, the luggage, and finding the rental car—in the rain. We were supposed to find the place where we were staying that night and then go to my godparents' house the next day, but I felt desperate. I couldn't find it, and something told me to just to go to my godparents' place and get my bearings. So I pulled off at their house, and Joseph was there, awake with a smile. He gave me a kiss and told me he loved me. Poet woke up in the car, so Tori brought her into the house, and Joseph got to see her. Then we left for the night.

By the next morning Joseph had started slipping away, and just days later he was gone.

I was always close to my godmother, and in the time since

Joseph passed away, our relationship has grown only deeper. Our love has continued to grow, and the moments we spend when we are together, up until the late-night hours talking, are some of the most precious in my life, and ones I hold closest to my heart. She is truly remarkable.

I wouldn't be who I am if it weren't for Bryten, Joseph, and all the other dear friends I've known and lost. They are all still alive in me and those who loved them—which is exactly what we tell our girls. Bryten's legacy is in the art he made and the lives he touched. Joseph was one of the most creative, brilliant, and passionate people you could ever meet. He left behind a lifetime of incredible work and family who love him endlessly. He loved life and every breath of beauty that he took in. He is still such a huge part of our lives and our children's; they wave to him in the sunset, and look up and see him in the stars—and remember that amazing, inspiring dash he spent with us.

Meeno

My godfather, Joseph, and me at my baby shower for Poet

* * *

S.P.S.

The dash between . . .

What have been your favorite moments in life? Take the time to write down your most special memories so far and how you will inspire yourself and your children to make the most of the dash in between. Today I was watching my husband holding our daughters, and I literally held that moment close to my heart throughout the afternoon. I thought about how that was part of my dash. It is so easy to rush through life, but I really try to take time to treasure the moments. When you feel yourself getting overwhelmed, take a beat and think about what is really important. When we look back thirty or forty years from now, will it be the one deadline we reflect on, or the morning we dropped our kids off late for school? No, it will be the laughter and tears, the first steps, the birthdays, the growing, the weddings, the love, and the people we shared our lives with.

What about those moments when our kids ask us about those whose dash has passed on?

My girls ask me hard questions all the time. I used to ask my mother a thousand questions and now my kids are doing the exact same thing with me. The other day at breakfast Poet asked me, "Mom, what happens when we die?" I took a breath and then I said that everyone believes in different things.

Some people think that we become stars in the sky and other people believe that we go to another place, somewhere that is beautiful and where the skies have cotton candy clouds. She and her sister smiled softly and then ran off to play. Sometimes our kids ask us questions that are really tough for us to answer, but I truly believe that compassion can help them evolve into incredible people. All of these questions and wonders about their world are so pivotal to the essence of their being and the dash that they create along the way.

29

. . . .

Please and Thank You

Question of the day: What kinds of rules do you have in your house?

"My kids are toddler & preschool age. So our main rules are: be kind to each other, remember that the dog's water isn't a Little People pool, and no flipping off the back of the sofa."

—Amy

"No TV or computer on Sundays; dinner every night with everyone in the family; and no phone calls during meals; if my kids are slow to get out of bed for school in the morning, they must go to bed earlier that night; everyone must do their best to show respect for one another, otherwise they get in trouble."

—Irene

"The rules are pretty broad at our house: Love each other. Don't speak harsh words. Put your dirty clothes in the hamper. :) Share. Be helpful."

—JoyfulTxGal

"The kids have to try whatever food is put in front of them—at least one bite. No one gets called 'stupid.' Everyone gets a hug, kiss and 'I love you' from everyone before bed."

—Kelly F.

"Rules? Not enough! I'm going to end with that so that I don't incriminate myself lol!"

—Lisa U.

As you have probably figured out by now, my mom's house was a totally free-spirited Nirvana kind of place. No one had what you would call a traditional job, and no one kept what you would call traditional hours. We often ate dinner cross-legged on the floor, we had a houseful of animals, and we almost always had a houseful of people—and nobody was waiting for an invitation. But manners were important to my mom—at least the really important ones, like saying "please" and "thank you." And even when we were sitting on the floor to eat, we always took a few quiet moments to appreciate our blessings.

My dad's manners . . . well, they were a little looser. I remember one time he came to visit me on the set of *Punky*, and we went to the cafeteria for lunch. My mom and I sat down with a woman who worked on the set, and when Dad walked up, he started eating the french fries right off of that woman's plate. And just to clarify—my dad didn't know her at all. They'd never met! Yet there he was, devouring her fries. Perfectly mannered, no, but my dad's heart was always in the right place. And to me, that's the important thing. My dad always tried to make you feel good when you were with him, even if he sometimes ate fries off the plates of strangers.

HAPPY CHAOS

There are two kinds of people in this world: the ones who usually make you feel a little worse about yourself after you've been with them, and the ones who always manage to make you feel a little better. Even small acts of generosity can make a huge difference. Back when I was a teenager trying to make a new reputation for myself in Hollywood, I went to an audition with Francis Ford Coppola for a film version of *On the Road*. Auditions are always difficult, but when you're a self-conscious teenager, they can be a nightmare. Everything about you is being dissected, from your work to your face, and you can end up feeling totally unworthy.

But Francis wasn't like that at all. He asked me all about a recent role (I was starring in an incredibly intense play about Hitler's niece at the time). He then asked me to read him a poem I had written. He wanted to hear all about my obsession with gangster movies, and all of my interests, loves, and passions. He must have spent an hour with me. This was around the time that I was working on my very first screenplay (*Blood and Brotherhood*), and he couldn't possibly have known what a huge impact a conversation with the brilliant Francis Ford Coppola would have on me. For that hour there didn't seem to be anything in the world more important to him than our conversation. I've always held that experience close to my heart, and I've tried really hard to pass on that same sort of kindness—and to give people my complete attention when they are talking about something close to their heart.

We all have a choice in this life to build each other up or break each other down. Jason and I try to teach our girls to be builders. We teach them about kindness and paying it forward. We talk about how we can make the world a better place. And we get them involved in really concrete ways—whether it's my work with the Alzheimer's Foundation, or teaching them about their grandfather's work with the civil rights movement.

Of course, manners are important, too. I've tried to teach my girls not to steal french fries off of strangers' plates, how to sit at the dinner table (although often they prefer to sit on it instead of at it), and to cover their mouths when they cough, and I'm happy to say that Poet and Jagger have become total champs at saying "please" and "thank you," just like my mother taught me when I was little. What makes me proudest of them isn't how automatically they say it, though—it's how deeply they feel it.

* * *

S.P.S.

Speaking of table manners . . .

Is this scenario familiar to you? Everyone sits down to a lovingly prepared meal, and one or more children look at their plates in horror and refuse to eat. Mom and Dad are mortified, whoever prepared the meal is upset, and what's the right thing to do? So many parents struggle with this, and I'm incredibly sympathetic. I have never been a parent who forces my kids to sit at the table and finish every last bite, but I know people who have. I think that when kids stress out about food, they are less likely to eat it. At the same time, you don't want to give them ten other options so that it becomes a habit. Usually I will ask nicely for them to eat what they like of it. If I feel like they still haven't gotten enough, I will give them a little snack before bed and then the next day they are back to eating their whole meal. Figuring out how they sometimes test us is important, and the better we understand that, the easier time we will have with picky eaters.

With very picky eaters, preparing things they love while introducing one or two new things is a great idea. Then they can experiment with a spoonful of something new as opposed to a whole plate of it.

Being polite . . .

Talk to your kids about being polite and how a little kindness goes a long way. Making eye contact and being sincere when speaking with others is really important to me. I think leading by example and healthy, subtle reminders are helpful. I like to remind them on a playdate, for example, that it is not just when they are saying good-bye at somebody's house that they should say "thank you"—it's important to be appreciative and respectful of others throughout the visit.

Just remember that no one's perfect . . .

Since we're talking about manners and thoughtfulness, I want to take this opportunity to confess a serious moral failing on my part. I'm not kidding—this is really shameful. I like to think that I'm a kind and generous person, and I really try to be a good friend, a good parent, a loving wife . . . but I am the *worst* with thank-you notes. I don't know what my problem is. Sometimes I even go to the trouble of writing out a note, but then I never manage to get it addressed and stamped.

So let's make this official: For everyone who has ever given my child a birthday present . . . thank you. And for anyone who has ever given me a birthday present . . . thank you. And for every single person who has ever given me an engagement present, or a wedding present, or an anniversary present . . . THANK YOU. I treasure each and every one. And here's a promise—you never have to send me a thank-you note, either, not ever.

Anne Marie Fox

Jason and me with Demi and Ashton, two of the most kind and loving people in our lives

30

. . . .

Be My Baby

Question of the day: How do you most baby your babies?

"Lots of love, hugs, kisses & cuddles."

—Nicole P.

"I baby my babies by cuddling them. Even in public. My poor 11 year old son!"

—Ash

"Carry them, even though they are nearly as big as me. (They are only 5 and 1. I'm just tiny.)"

—Dana

"Weeeell, my 'babies' are 37 and almost-40 now, but still by trying to make things smooth for them."

—Jan

"Wrap up together on the couch for movies—especially *The Princess Bride*."

—Cari

My mom always tells me that I was her little girl for a short time, and then she shared me with the world. That has really stuck with me. She must be braver than I am, because I don't want to share my girls with the world. I want them home with me forever.

It was hard enough to send them off to preschool. Poet was shy at first, but now she runs through the door and doesn't even look back. Jagger is already headed in that direction, too, and she's my baby! Sometimes I just stare at my girls sleeping—their height, hair, how they're taking up the entire room, and how they are getting so big, so fast. I want to press a button and make time stop. But the genie is already out of the bottle. Poet is one hundred percent big girl now. Meanwhile, I'm in no rush to hurry Jagger out of her baby years. I'm like, want a bottle? Want your pacifier? No problem!

I think back to the crazy adventures I had when I wasn't much older than Poet, and I wonder how my mother managed not to have a total heart attack on a daily basis. One incident that really sticks out in my memory happened when I was doing *Punky*. I was probably eight at the time. I was a child spokesperson for the Just Say No to Drugs campaign, and Nancy Reagan was the chair, so she invited me to the White House Easter Egg Roll. When my mom, brother, and I got there the crowd of fans was gigantic, way bigger than we expected. In the enormous crowd, suddenly I lost sight of my mother. The next thing I knew, I was surrounded by these incredibly cool Secret Service guys who ushered me through the mob scene and into the White House. When my mom finally found me, I was in the Oval Office with my feet up on the table, eating Popeyes fried chicken. I wasn't a baby anymore.

I don't want to admit it to my girls, but some of the best experiences in my life happened when my parents weren't around, like at summer camp, which I *loved*. My mom exaggerated a little when I was five and said that I was already six, just so that I could go to sleepaway camp for two weeks. And from then until I was seventeen, I went every year. I even went back as a counselor. Now it blows my mind to realize that Poet is the same age I was when I went to sleepaway camp for the first time. I can't even imagine sending her yet!

Here I am arriving at summer camp with my sleeping bag and sunglasses, everything a tween needs!

Of course, my older brother Meeno was there, and I had Tori with me, too. That camp was so awesome. It doesn't exist anymore, which is so sad, because I really would send my girls there if I could. (In a few more years, when they're older!) It was in Calabasas, California, and I treasure every little memory. I remember the lanterns, the crafts we'd make, riding horses and dirt bikes, and going to dances. We'd run up and down the dunes at Point Dune, where the counselors would take us for overnight camping and tell us the most amazing stories. I remember my older friend, Chrissy, who'd pack all her stuff for the beach overnights in a black trash bag— including her curling iron. Of course, there were no outlets at the beach.

The boys and girls weren't separated at my camp (no wonder I loved it so much). There was this boy named Danny Wells who both Tori and I had huge crushes on. I swear, at age fourteen he had six-pack abs. So Tori and I spent one whole summer obsessing over him. Then the next summer, Danny and I got together. It was the full-on summer camp romance— sneaking away from the counselors and talking all night. I remember the song of that summer was the Bangles' "Eternal Flame," and that song still comes to mind when I think of Danny. Tori was beyond upset with me for hooking up with him, and it got so bad that she actually moved her bunk away from mine. When Tori got upset, our other friend Chrissy tried to figure out why Tori was so crushed about this guy. She said, "Tori, what's he into?" Tori said, "He's a wrestler." Chrissy's response? I will never forget this. She said, "Tori, he rolls around on the floor with another guy. You know what you need? You need a surfer."

I learned that and so much more when my mother was nowhere nearby. Then I would come home and tell my mom about all of my crazy adventures and it became a really beautiful bonding experience for us. Even if it is hard to let go a little bit, it will make our kids full of more experiences, awe, and wonder. I know the thought of my kids becoming teenagers is enough to make me cry, but every thread that comes loose, every growing pain that makes them stronger, can also build strength and trust between us and our children.

I'm happy to think of all the wonderful things my girls are going to experience—even if it makes me sad when I realize I won't always be there to see them. One of these days I know I'm going to have to set them free and share my girls with the world just like my mom did with me. Then Poet and Jagger can have their own adventures—without me. And I'll be here, waiting for them to come home and tell me everything. Or at least call.

I find myself saying every day, "You will always be Mommy's little baby forever." I say this over and over again, and I'm not sure if my kids like to hear it as much as I like to say it. It's probably my way of telling myself that no matter how far from the nest my kids wander, something will always bring them back. I just hope that wandering time doesn't come too fast.

* * *

S.P.S.

The letters to my little ones . . .

It's hard to watch our children grow up, but at the same time we want to encourage them to be their own people. Writing a letter is a great way to show your love throughout time. One of my favorite things to do is to write my girls letters at different stages in their lives. I tell them about the people they are and how much they inspire me. I seal the envelope, and one day I hope that we get to read them together or that they will read them on their own. I want them to be able to reflect on the children that they were and see that throughout the different steps in their lives, Mom and Dad were there for them and loved them always with an open heart.

Encouraging a little independence . . .

You might not be ready to send your five-year-old to camp, but your five-year-old can help choose clothes and even have fun getting themselves dressed. Just the other day Poet said, "Mom, I'm going to get myself dressed." I replied, "Okay." She came out in a colorful outfit that she had put together herself. It was unique and she was proud. I complimented her on what a great job she had done, and she felt really good about it. I think being aware of the power we have to build our children's spirit is so important to how we raise our little ones. And even if it is hard when your kid walks in with hot pink cowboy boots, mismatched socks, and a crazy-looking top, it's better to make them feel good about their choice and enjoy it for a little while than to knock them down. That free spirit is an amazing thing and can really help define the people they grow into. Who knows, you may have a future fashion designer in the making.

Allowing them to be creative and helpful in the kitchen . . .

Last night the girls and I made a big feast for Jason. I asked Poet if she could help me make a Caprese salad. I then washed and sliced the tomatoes and basil. I gave her mozzarella and green olives to decorate the plate. She pulled a chair over to the counter, washed her hands, and started creating the most beautiful Caprese salad I have ever seen. I didn't try to change what she was doing or constantly correct her. I allowed her creative freedom to make it her own. She was so happy with it when she was finished, and both she and Jagger were thrilled when Jason came home from work and his face lit up seeing what they had created. So whether it is having your kids help in the kitchen, clean their rooms, help around the house, or create their own fashions, let them exercise a little independence while allowing them to do it in their own unique way.

Courtesy of the author

My amazing achievements at summer camp :) lol

31

Rated PG

Question of the day: How do you plan on telling your kids where babies come from and at what age?

"I explained generally when my kids were about 10. But they don't know the specifics about sex yet. I don't think they are mature enough to hear that yet. I think it depends on the child though. Some might be ready to hear sooner than others."

—Sheila

"Straightforward, lots of love and care, and when the conversations with my children lead to those topics."

—Nicole P.

"Uh, I have an 11-year-old boy so my husband has already started the series of 'talks' with him. He will tell our sons and I will tell our daughters. So far, whenever any of them have asked a question about where babies come from, I tell them simple truthful answers."

—Irene

"When they are ready. The first time my son asked he was 5. I told him. I didn't use technical terms, I explained it in language he could understand. I did the same when he asked two years later, and last year when he asked I told him again. That time it stuck."

—Allen

I had endless adventures as a kid, and I got to do amazing things and meet fascinating people. No matter how much I did and saw, though, I still felt and acted like a kid. It's all thanks to my mother, who always worked incredibly hard to protect my innocence. When I was traveling for *Punky*, Tori usually came along with me, and instead of taking us shopping or out to a fancy restaurant, my mom would find out where the nearest carnival was and take us there.

I hope to do the same for my girls—expose them to lots of wonderful things, while not rushing them to grow up any faster than they already are. I know that it's easier said than done, though. I was at a party a few weeks ago and there was a nine-year-old girl all decked out in the height of tween fashion, carrying a purse and making calls on a cell phone. I was kind of horrified, but then I asked myself, *What about when my girls are a little older and they go someplace without me—will I want them to be able to call me, and will I give them a cell phone to use?* I guess I'll find out when the time comes!

I've always said that Poet is five going on fifteen at times, so I already know what it's like to gently put on the brakes. When we go into a clothing store, of course she gravitates to the brightest, most sparkly outfits, and she went through a stage where she absolutely refused to wear pants. So finally I convinced her to wear leggings under her bright, spinny skirts. I'd love to get her into a pair of jeans, but who am I to squelch her free expression, especially when it comes to clothes? Especially since my idea of getting dressed when I was little was to decorate myself head to toe in finger paints and wear nothing but a pair of roller skates.

My friend Danny Masterson will never let me forget that I'm responsible for robbing him of just a little bit of his innocence way back in preschool. Let's just say that I had a bit of a problem with underwear. Meaning: I refused to wear any. And I didn't really like pants, either. In fact, the only type of clothing that my mother could get me to wear without complaint was oversize T-shirts—and nothing else. The preschool agreed to allow me to go to school dressed like that, but given the lack of underwear, they asked my mother to make sure that my T-shirts were especially long. Right around that time, the boys at school launched "Flip-up Fridays," when they'd flip up the girls' skirts. Danny said he got his first

Courtesy of the author

My incredible friend Danny Masterson and me at five years old. I still have the picture in the same seventies frame on my mantel.

introduction to female anatomy when he flipped up my T-shirt.

Our kids are learning all kinds of lessons from the world around them—and some take us by surprise. One of my favorite movies is *Grease*—I have an obsession with both *Grease* and *Grease 2* that has lived on through my girls. Remember in the "Happy Birthday" chapter when I told you about Poet's fifth-birthday party? It had a *Grease* theme and was as fun for me as it was for them. But even I gulped a little when we watched *Grease* together for the first time and we got to the make-out part (which I had conveniently forgotten all about).

Poet has seen enough kissing in movies to have some ideas about how and why it's done. These days her main response to the concept is "yuck," but those curious wheels are already starting to turn in her head. A month or so ago she was riding along in the backseat of our car when suddenly she asked us, "How did you and Mommy have me?" So Jason said that he and I love each other, and then we made her together. That seemed to satisfy her for the time being. Then Jason and I shared a look as we wondered what our future conversations of this nature with our children would be like. Both of us sat in the car staring ahead, not saying a word. I began having flashbacks to my own childhood and all of my questions. *This is it*, I thought to myself. *Just a short time ago I was the kid asking my mom where babies came from, and in the blink of an eye, my own kids are asking me the same thing.* And just like that, I became my mother. We all do, if only for a moment at a time. That person we never think we will be like when we grow up is the person we see in our own reflection. How did that happen so fast? And how do our kids grow up so fast?

* * *

S.P.S.

. . . .

The big talk . . .

I think it may be a myth that there's one "big talk" about sex that you need to have with your kids. Maybe it's really lots of little talks, and they happen when your kid is ready (and yes, even if *you're* not ready). How do you know your kid is ready? When they're asking questions is one good sign. But you don't necessarily want to assume that this is the only time you should talk to them. Maybe there's a situation in a storybook, movie, or television show that you can use to explain a small concept. Or maybe you have a friend who's pregnant, and that's an opportunity for a talk. I think it's best to keep the lines of communication open. Thinking of outside-the-box ways to talk to your kids about subjects that can be sensitive for us is always helpful as well. When I talk about body image with my little ones, often I will refer to an Italian painting or piece of artwork that shows different shapes and sizes. I think the most important thing is to try not to make your children feel ashamed about their curiosity. When our kids see that there's no shame in asking questions or being confused—and that there are no shameful subjects—they're much more likely to raise their own questions when they have them. This allows us to try to help them have a better understanding while encouraging them to feel a comfort in confiding in us.

There's no such thing as a stupid question . . .

As you know by now, I'm a big believer in open communication in a family. It really affects every area of our lives as
parents. We want our kids to feel that they can tell us
anything—and that they can ask us anything. But that doesn't
happen overnight—you have to work on it every day. Our lives
are so busy that sometimes we really have to make a point of
talking to each other and truly listening. Make sure your kids
know that you always want them to come to you with questions. I say to my kids all the time that there are no stupid
questions, and I think it is important to continue bringing
that up. If they don't learn things from home, they will pick it
up somewhere else. So it's better that they have an accurate
understanding from you than to get misinformation.

32

. . . .

Crushes

Question of the day: Who was your first love, and how old were you?

> "My best friend growing up, Steve. We were 11. I never told him though. He was too good of a friend, and I was scared."
>
> —AnaLiesa

> "As a very young child (4-5 years old) I was in love with two Turkish twins who were in my school! I imagined I would fly away to their country with them (both!) on a helicopter with their mommy on board . . ."
>
> —Amelie

> "My first love was a guy named Joe and I was 13. He was my best friend and we were together for 2 years. I still miss him to this day."
>
> —Lisa M.

"When I was in 6th grade—I finally went on a real date with him when I was 15 and he was having an acid trip the whole time. I demanded to be taken home and that crush was OVER!"

—Jessica

"My first love was Mike at the age of 17. He was gorgeous, sweet, and it didn't last as long as I wished it would."

—Sherill

It is hard to talk about my love of boys without a time line because I really was that boy-crazy. For as far back as I can remember, I always loved boys. Even before I could talk, my big brother's friends would come over to visit and give me bear hugs or tickle me as I turned beet red with shyness. I loved the attention. By the time I was five, I was pretending Danny Masterson was my boyfriend. He was my best friend, and we would do sleepovers on a regular basis. I even went to New York to stay with his family and I slept on the lower bunk of his trundle bed. I still remember those adorable little boy blankets, all blue and snuggly, while my best buddy/future husband slept above me. To this day he is still one of my closest friends. My husband and he are close as well. Funny how things turn out.

By the time I was about six, I really fell in love. It was Valentine's Day, or maybe we were just cutting heart-shaped cards, but there I sat in the trailer that the kids would hang out in on our set school of *Little Shots* when he walked in. His name was Joey Lawrence, and he had the hottest bowl cut I had ever seen. It kind of moved all at once when he walked up the stairs into the room. He had this smile and his eyes sparkled. I think I may have heard birds chirping that day. He smiled; I smiled back. That young love would last for years off and on. And as fate would have it, I did *Punky Brewster* at the same time he was on *Gimme a Break!*

Lucky for me, in the eighties every show on NBC was like a family, and for every NBC special all the shows would come together to perform. Whether it was singing beside Nell Carter and Don Johnson, or dancing beside Betty White and Michael J. Fox, our paths all inevitably crossed. I would bump into Joan Collins while someone put on my ChapStick backstage, or get a big hug from one of the cast members from *The Facts of Life*. When I say it was like a family at NBC, I really mean it. But back to my love of boys . . .

Sondra Peluce

Here I am with the Lawrences and Tori at Venice Beach, way back in the day

Joey and I would cross paths over the years. Our families became very close, and the next thing we knew, we were off to

Finland to film *The Andy Williams Christmas Special* together with about a dozen other kids, listening to Wham! By the time I turned eight, I considered him my full-on boyfriend. I will never forget the glorious night when we were both at the opening of *Captain Eo* at Disneyland. It was on the Pirates of the Caribbean ride when I lay my head gently against his bowl cut that I fell in love for the first time. Throughout those years we stayed friends. We would run through the Beverly Center and hide under the benches, always my favorite way to spend a Saturday night. But by the time he started *Blossom*, our love had faded. After a visit to his home in the Valley, his parents drove me home one night and I knew something had changed, although I would carry the memory of our love for years to come.

My first intense, heart-pounding infatuation came when I was eight. It was the moment I met Andy Gibb. To this day, I can still smell his cologne and hear his voice. He did two episodes of *Punky Brewster*, and my love only grew as we worked together. He had the biggest heart of anyone I had ever met, and he showed me such kindness. He wore these bright red leather pants and he made me feel like I was a queen. After we finished taping the second episode, he asked me to come to his room because he had something special for me. I walked in, my heart pounding through my chest, and he told me to close my eyes. He wore the same black sequined jacket on *Punky* that he had worn when he hosted *Solid Gold*, and as my eyes were shut tight, he wrapped it around me and told me that it now belonged to me. I still have the jacket to this day. A few months ago, I was standing in a store with my daughters when I heard the song that he sang to me on *Punky* playing. It was a song I had searched for over the years and now someone else was singing it, but it was the same song. My heart melted and tears fell down my cheeks. My girls said, "Mommy, what's wrong?" I replied, "Someone very special once sang this to me." When we got home, we curled up on the couch and I played them the clip of him singing to me on YouTube. The video was grainy and old-school, but if you looked closely at my face, you could see how in love with him I was.

By eight and a half there was R. J. Williams, who was the bad boy on *Punky*, and he stole my heart early on. We would kiss on-set and we didn't care who saw us. People thought it was cute. I guess you could say we taught each other how to French-kiss, although we didn't know what it meant and I certainly didn't understand what was French about it. By age nine, I had moved on to Chad Allen, who was on *Punky* with me for a few episodes. We would spend weekends at each other's houses, and Tori would count how many minutes we would cuddle for. Chad was great—we went on years later to play brother and sister together in a movie in Thailand with Pat Morita and became great friends. We would

Courtesy of the author

The gorgeous and lovable Andy Gibb and me on the set of *Punky*. I get flustered just looking at this picture. That was the black sequined jacket he gave me, and I still adore it.

listen to Depeche Mode and the Cure, but the spark was no longer there. Chad went on to like boys as well, but he was a gentle and great early boyfriend.

Here I am with Charlie on Henry's couch. My cheeks were burning red and I was having a full-blown crush attack.

At about ten years old, I was sent home one day from the set because of how boy-crazy I was. Charlie Sheen and I had the same publicist, and this was around the time *Wall Street* had come out. I was looking particularly messy that day, disheveled from playing rough on-set. I was rehearsing a scene with Cherie as she whispered, "Is that Charlie Sheen in the bleachers?" I looked up and there he was, sitting in the empty audience seats, in a black suit jacket, white T-shirt, and sunglasses. I was in total awe. After the scene was over, we met. I was so flustered that I turned bright red. He sat next to me on the big seventies couch in Henry's living room and put his arm around me for some pictures. I could barely contain myself. I could feel my cheeks burning, and my chest about to explode. He was very sweet, and as we spoke, random people began coming up to me to check my temperature, putting their hands on my forehead, thinking I was sick. *No, I'm not sick; I'm having a full-blown internal crush freak-out*, I thought to myself. The studio nurse came down and determined that I had far too high a fever to continue working. It was the first and only time I was sent home from set—all because of a crush temperature. Awesome. If I was going to keep having surprise visitors, I would need to work on hiding my crush fevers. That one lasted for a few weeks, at least until Johnny Depp showed up for a visit.

At eleven, I worked with Mark-Paul Gosselaar for the first time, and we hit it off beautifully. He had dirty-blond hair and green eyes. He was a sweetheart. I put his head shot up in my room, and I guess you could say he was my boyfriend from that very moment—although the term was used loosely, as we had only hugged at that point. There was a place in Hollywood called Alfie's Soda Pop Club where kids would hang out, dance, and drink soda. It was awesome, like a party every weekend. It was at one of these parties, while the DJ was playing LL Cool J's "I Need Love," that I remember kissing Mark-Paul for the first time. He was chewing a green minty gum and it was very sweet and romantic. He lived in Valencia and I lived in Burbank, thirty miles apart, and a long-distance relationship was not in the cards, but on a few occasions over the years, I remember us hanging out while my mom drove us around looking outside at the moonlight. He was kind and loving. But by the time I did *Saved by the Bell*, he was off with some beautiful girl and I was kind of interested in Mario Lopez. Mario was super sexy and had the biggest biceps you have ever seen. Years later, Mark Paul and I did a movie together and laughed for days about our history and how far we had come.

By the time I turned thirteen, I had my first real taste of a bad boy. His name was Balthazar Getty, and he quickly became one of my closest friends. We would stay up late talking on the phone, and he introduced me to all of the best music. He exuded cool and was just tough enough to make your heart race. One night he told me that he was going to come to visit me. He was over the hill in Hollywood and I was deep in the Valley. He said not to worry, that he would get there. The next thing I knew, he and his friend were pulling up to my house on his friend's brother's dirt bike they had stolen. Aw, the lengths we will go to at that age. After hours of hanging out, they headed back and got pulled over by the police. Thirteen and fearless. I loved that about Balt.

When it came time for my junior prom, I had only one person I wanted as my date, and it was Balthazar. He showed up to my house with a gray suit and a cool tie. It was a hot getup, very mature for his fourteen years of age. He proceeded to get me into all kinds of fun trouble at the prom, and then we headed to Malibu, where we ate chocolate cake at Gladstones. Before we got to our friend's car, he said, "Hey, let's take a walk down to the beach." We all headed down to the water, and, in true bad-boy fashion, he picked me up and carried me into the ocean with him. There we were, decked out in all of our prom clothes, swimming in the Pacific Ocean, and it was awesome. All these years later I am still friends with Balthazar and his wife, Rosetta. As I stood at his daughter's birthday party a few months ago and saw him give his

Sondra Peluce

Me and Balthazar getting ready to leave for junior prom. He looks super cool, and me? Let's just say I would like to go back in time and fix my hair.

daughter her present, I couldn't help but smile and laugh to myself. It was a dirt bike.

There is one boy who my youth would not have been complete without. His name was Brian Green. We went through every stage together, and he was always there for me. Looking back, if I had to choose who always had my back when I was a teenager—a person I could depend on if I ever felt like I was falling down—it was Brian. He came from a great family, and I knew him from the time he was awkward through his transformation into a total heartthrob. He was the first boy I knew who got his own place and bought super-cool cars.

I could literally gush about Brian and all of our moments for a whole chapter, but instead I will keep it short and sweet. Our lives were filled with funny and playful moments, like the time he picked me up and my brother tried to scare him off while wearing red long johns, or cruising around in his gorgeous old convertible sports car. Playing pool at all hours. But one memory stands out to me more than all the others with Brian. One night, we were sitting talking, and in our conversation I said, "Hey, why don't you pick me up from school one day?" He said, "Sure." We went back and forth and I told him he would flake and he said he wouldn't—you know the way you flirt as a kid. The next day, as I got out from my Catholic school (I'm not Catholic but I loved the uniforms), I walked out to see Brian sitting in his car with music pumping. This was at the height of *90210* and all of the cheerleaders with their pom-poms and pleated skirts stared in shock and awe as I

Sondra Peluce

No words . . . I mean, really? I think our expression says it all.

jumped into the passenger seat and we cruised off. If I had to choose one of many moments when I felt most popular and on top of the world as a teenager, I would have to say that this was definitely one of mine.

At about fourteen years old, I had the biggest crush of my entire life. I was in New York doing a funny talk show called *Girl Talk* with Sarah Michelle Gellar when I went to interview New Kids on the

Block. They were at the height of their fame at the time, and every girl in the world was in love with them. It was on the stage that I saw the most handsome boy I had ever laid eyes on. His name was Mark Wahlberg. As my luck would have it, our paths would cross again back in LA at Universal Studios a few months later. We were backstage when Mark's brother Donnie introduced us. My heart immediately burst out of my chest. It was at this moment that I felt butterflies and flushed beyond words. I mentioned that I needed a date for an Emmy party the next night. Donnie immediately offered Mark, who smiled and said that he would love to be my date. The next night we met on Sunset Boulevard at a hotel where the party was taking place. I met him at the front of the hotel, decked out in my nineties best: black catsuit dress with a skirt and even shorts (yes, I said shorts) along with knee-high socks and platform shoes. He had on a blue floral shirt with jeans. As we walked in, photographers took photos and we puckered up. My heart was racing. We sat in a corner and talked all night. The next day he and his friend came to our house in Burbank. We played pool and laughed, and I was giddy with excitement. My stepdad let us take his gold Honda motorcycle for a drive up the street. I remember Prince playing through my head as we stopped to look at the lights in the valley.

My crazy crush on Mark lasted for a long time. One of my favorite memories was going to Boston with one of my best friends, Maggie, and climbing into Mark's big car with pumping speakers and listening to his Marky Mark and the Funky Bunch demo on the car stereo. This was pre–Calvin Klein, pre-fame, and I was crazy about him. His smile was enough to make any girl fall head over heels. He had all of the talent inside, and he was destined to turn it into something amazing.

Sondra Peluce

Mark Wahlberg and me on my stepdad's motorcycle. I was so crazy about that Boston boy.

There were the best friends who turned into crushes and then turned back into friends. There were the crushes whose lives ended too early, and those that lasted for years. Who would have ever thought a boy-crazy girl like me, who seemed to fall in love with a new guy every week, would settle down with the love of her life at such a young age? All of the practice over those years must have really helped me to open my heart when the time was right. By the time I turned twenty, I had fallen in love with my biggest crush of all, and now here we are, over fourteen years later. Who says that crushes can't turn into true love?

* * *

S.P.S.

. . . .

Crushes . . .

Take a moment for yourself to reflect on your childhood crushes, close your eyes, and savor the nostalgia of it all. How did that person or people inspire who you are today? Now get prepared to support your little ones when that day comes, because we all know that no matter how much we try to slow down time, it will happen, and, boy, when it does, watch out!

33

- - - - - - - - - - - - -

Wild Child

Question of the day: What is the most rebellious thing you did as a teenager?

"My dad told me to drop college, get a job he liked and cut my hair, or he'd throw me out. My wife told me to just stay out all night and then come back the next evening. It worked. That was really it."

—Allen

"I went on a week long road trip with friends instead of going to school."

—Amelia

"I ran away from home once . . . Well kind of. I ran to my favorite spot, which was 20 feet from the back door. Everyone kept calling out my name but I was upset and needed to cool off. When I came back, I got grounded for three weeks."

—AnaLiesa

"I dyed my hair blue."

—Katie

Poet might be only five, but sometimes she acts like a teenager. Every once in a while I hear a little tone in her voice. She'll say, "Mo-om," while rolling her eyes when I've said something embarrassing to her. The first time your kids roll their eyes at you, you don't know whether to laugh or cry. When I remember the stuff I did as a teenager, first I think, *My poor mother*, and then I think, *Oh my God, we are so in for it.*

As I've mentioned, my mom always had an incredibly liberal attitude with her children. She basically said, "If you're going to experiment, do it at home." And it's funny, because I think that is one of the reasons my brother and I turned out so well—because our mom was so open. It just never seemed like much of a forbidden thrill. Sure, I had my wild-child moments, but I got them out of my system pretty early.

Once my mom and I went to New York for a big event. I was probably sixteen at the time, and I left my dress at the airport—and I didn't notice until we'd gotten all the way to the hotel. Mom was annoyed with me, and since it was already late, she told me to go to bed. She got back in a taxi and went to the airport to get my dress.

Meanwhile, a young actor friend of mine was in New York. He sneaked me out of the hotel room and I got totally stoned with him for the first time. I remember that in this dazed and confused state we thought it would be super fun to go running up and down escalators all over Manhattan.

Of course, all the while this was happening, my mom thought I was fast asleep at the hotel. Finally I raced back to the room, reeking of pot smoke, and knowing my mom was going to be back any second to check on me. So I jumped in the shower and washed my mouth out. When I caught my reflection in the mirror, I was really flushed. I was just lucky the room was dark when my mom came in and I was deep under the covers, pretending to be asleep.

When I was seventeen, my mom didn't even blink when I told her that I wanted to go on tour with my friend Danny O'Connor, who was in House of Pain. I used to carry a little video camera with me wherever I went, filming everything, almost like a video journal. My mom totally encouraged me to chase my inspiration, so when I decided I wanted to do a documentary on House of Pain, Mom agreed and Meeno came

Meeno

along with me. It was a blast, and I became good friends with the whole group and everyone on the road in the process.

One night we were out shooting really late and I stayed over at my friend Danny's house. The next morning, I left to go back home in my little black Jetta and accidentally went full speed into reverse, slamming into the back of Danny's old hatchback. His car

Danny O'Connor and me playing around for the camera

was fine; mine was totally trashed. So I ran inside and yelled, "I need stickers!" Then I plastered the back of my car with House of Pain stickers everywhere—like that was going to hide the damage from my mother. One look at my patch job, and even I knew that there was no way my mom wasn't going to see that huge dent. She was easygoing, but she wasn't *that* easygoing.

I was also very good friends with Cathy Moriarty during this time, who owned Mulberry Street Pizzeria, and I used to hang out there all the time. So instead of going home to face my mother with my wrecked Jetta, I went over to show Cathy the damage. Joey, another one of my friends who worked there, knew a place where we could get my car fixed—for seven hundred dollars. Oh my God, there was no way I could go to my mother for seven hundred dollars to fix the car. Then I'd have to tell her how I crashed it in the first place. So Joey fronted me the money, the body shop fixed my car, and I worked with my friends at Mulberry Street Pizzeria to pay off my debt. I don't know if my mother ever knew the real reason why I was flipping pizzas for a few months after that.

There were so many crazy things that I did with my friends back then, because let's face it—teenagers are teenagers. But even when I was at my wackiest, I always came home. And I always knew that there really wasn't anything I couldn't tell my mom. Maybe I didn't tell her about the car . . . or that night I ran through Manhattan with the munchies . . . but I told her the really important stuff, always. And I want my girls to do the same thing. Of course, we'll give them all the really important parental advice when the time comes—never drive drunk, always call home if they need a ride, how to be safe and take care of themselves.

The girls might roll their eyes at us when we tell them these things, but I know that they'll get the message. We'll leave our lessons for them like a trail of bread crumbs in the forest. And then when they have their wild-child moments, they'll always be able to find their way home again.

* * *

S.P.S.

Parent, friend, or both . . .

I really feel like my mother was always my mom first. I knew a lot of kids growing up whose mothers wanted to be their best friends, but who were not really there for them as a parent. It was important for my mom to feel like her role as my mother was clear while still maintaining an openness and trust between us that made me feel like she was a friend I could turn to.

I think it is important to be a parent and for our kids to have an understanding of who we are and what the role of parent means in the family dynamic. Our kids feel safe and protected when they know they can depend on the person or people closest in their lives. I also think that the open line of communication between us and our children will create a friendship and bond with our kids that they will cherish. When they are older, I would love to sit and have coffee with my girls while reading our favorite books, but more importantly I want them to know that they can always come to me and that I am going to look out for them as their parent and that there are boundaries that we each must respect.

We each have a wild child inside of us . . .

If you're a new parent, it may feel really early to be thinking about these things, but it's never too early to figure out what kind of parent you want to be when those moments come—and we all know they will—when your kid is being a wild child. Reflect back to when you were young. What were the best lessons you ever learned and who taught them to you? Write down the things that most helped you and the areas where you wish that you could have had more support. I think some of the best lessons can come out of our own experiences. Also ask yourself, how did your parents handle certain situations? Would you have handled them differently?

Don't be afraid to repeat yourself . . .

When you're talking to your child about how to handle certain dangers of the world—whether it is to look both ways before they cross the street, or not to talk to strangers, or not to drink and drive—don't be surprised if your child looks away and insists they know all of that already. Sometimes, as parents, we have to be repetitive and even annoying to get a point across to our kids. Especially when their wild child comes out at a very young age.

34

. . . .

It Takes Time to Save the World

Question of the day: What is something that you have always wanted to do but have been too afraid to try?

"Culinary school."

—Cari

"World travel—not sure how to handle it with the kids."

—Nicole P.

"Maybe sky dive, but I really don't think I would ever have the guts to jump out of a plane."

—Irene

"I have always wanted to learn Sign Language, but have not gotten around to it. I wouldn't say that I am afraid to try it, but rather that I want to have the time that I will need to devote to it, so that I can master it."

—Nicole A.G.

grew up believing I could do anything, and I married a man who's totally supportive of every new and crazy idea I come up with. So of course, we want our girls to know that they can do anything, too.

A few weeks ago at school, Poet was out on the playground with her friends when she announced to the school's director, "We're superheroes and we're saving the world." So the director said, "Great, when will you be finished saving the world?" Then Poet gave her a look that said, *Hey lady, you can't rush these things,* and said with a little exasperation, "We're working on it! It takes time to save the world."

I would love to save the world—or at least make it a little better for my girls and future generations. For me, the first baby step in that direction was starting my company, the Little Seed. My friend Paige and I had both been searching the globe looking for healthy, organic alternatives for our kids, and had found it incredibly difficult to find the products we wanted for our little ones. We knew that if we were feeling this way, then there were probably millions of other families feeling the same. We were two moms who wanted to do something from our hearts, something that allowed us to be with our children and make a difference at the same time—so we decided to start our own company.

We tracked down the best possible organic products from baby bottles to toys, bedding, clothing, and any other healthy alternatives that we loved for our own kids. Within a month of opening the Little Seed, a huge number of children's toys were recalled, and we were suddenly thrust into the roles of eco mamas. Numerous news outlets showed up at our doorstep asking us what BPA meant, and asking questions about phthalates and toxins. Here we were discovering all of these incredible alternatives ourselves, and being given a voice and a platform to share that knowledge with others. Parents would come into our store and write us letters telling us about their favorite products. I have always believed that the mission of the Little Seed is so much bigger than Paige and me. It is a movement for families everywhere.

My partner in the Little Seed, Paige, and me hanging out at my house

Within a year we developed our own line of colorful organics and raw cotton clothing. I became a proud designer. At first I knew nothing about the garment industry and I had never gone to school for design, but here I was sketching baby pants and T-shirts. I would sit in front of color palettes with the girls and we would pick out colors together. It became a true family affair.

Paige and I had big dreams for the Little Seed—and the

biggest was to have our own aisle at Target. Then, about two years after we opened our shop in Los Angeles, there we were, our faces on more than a thousand endcaps across the country at Target with our bright and colorful line. This didn't happen overnight. It took tons of hard work, lots of flying back and forth to Minneapolis, and endless hours of designing, but we did it together. Our dream of making organics affordable for every parent and sharing our mission with the world came true. It was an amazing, brilliant, sometimes rocky, but incredibly creative journey . . . and if we knew then what we know now, we may have been too scared even to begin. Ignorance can be bliss!

Of course, a job that was supposed to be something we could do easily from home with our kids on our hips has turned into a huge endeavor, and sometimes Paige and I have to laugh that we thought we'd have so much flexibility with a company like this. We're flexible, all right—especially when we're up at all hours of the night working long after our kids are in bed. But I wouldn't trade it. The truth is, I love having ten things going on at once, and I love watching how this little seed that we planted has grown into a big tree with branches and roots all over the place. The Little Seed isn't just a store anymore; it's a whole community, and I couldn't be happier. So to all moms and dads out there: If you have a crazy idea rolling around in your head—something you've always wanted to try, a company you want to start, a product you want to invent, a T-shirt you want to design—I say, go for it. And if it might make the world a better place? All the better!

* * *

S.P.S.

As we say at the Little Seed, a little eco goes a long way. . . .

Here are just a few super-easy things you can do to make your family, your home, and the world a little healthier:

- Take walks with your family.

- Shut off the water whenever you can as opposed to running it for a long time. Poet always tells me if I am wasting water. I'm so proud of her.

- Bring your own reusable bags to the market.

- Turn off the lights when you leave a room—or the house.

- Recycle.

- Take your shoes off indoors (you would be amazed how much toxic stuff comes into the house on your shoes).

- Use natural, nontoxic cleaning products. Vinegar and water is an awesome option.

- Buy organic whenever possible.

- Buy local—make a fun weekly trip of visiting your nearest farmers' market.

- Switch to energy-efficient appliances, if you can and it is within your budget.

- Reduce waste—buy less, throw away less, and donate what you can't use.

- Reuse your kids' clothes. Nothing is cooler than secondhand.

- Have a get-together with your girlfriends to change up your latest fashion. Everyone brings the clothes that they no longer wear and puts them in a pile in the center of the room. Whatever doesn't get traded goes to Goodwill or the charity of your choice. This is a super-fun way to celebrate with your friends and do something positive for others and our planet at the same time

The joys of multitasking . . .

Working from home is amazing, but sometimes it is tough and I don't want my kids ever to feel like they are getting forty or fifty percent of me; I want them to get the whole package. So I am trying to be better about it. I realized recently that if I set some boundaries, it made it better on all of us. A few months ago I noticed that sometimes the problem for them isn't that I have to work; it's that I seem distracted. Now I make sure I set aside time just for the kids. If they're pulling on me to stop working, I might say, "Okay, in twenty minutes I'm going to stop, and then it's Mommy Time." And during that time they have my total, undivided attention. We bake, do a bath, cook, draw, or make lunch and talk. No phone, no e-mail. Then, when Mommy Time is over, it's back to work for a while. And because my girls know that when I am with them they have me one hundred percent, it's become a lot easier to tell them when it's Work Time.

Following your dreams . . .

I really do believe that each one of us has the power to make our dreams come true. I think it is very easy for us to get caught up in our everyday lives, but if there is something that you have always wanted to do or try, go for it. It is never too late to follow your dreams or dive into a project that inspires you. We have our responsibilities, and it is important to make sure that we take care of them, but we should still stay inspired, create, and refuel our spirits.

35

. . . .

Welcome Back, Virgil Frye

Question of the day: What is your favorite memory of your parents from growing up?

"Catching them dancing in the kitchen."

—Kelly F.

"When I was very little I remember my mother rocking me to sleep. I used to love that. I remember being chased by the neighbor's dogs and my father running out from the garage to save me. He stood there like a tower of strength, and the dogs which had been unstoppable monsters ran away. In one moment he had been so powerful and in the next he was holding me and wiping away my tears."

—Allen

"Their happy faces when they used to take me and my sister to the beach every summer. They were proud somehow to grant us these great holidays by the seaside and so delighted to see us amazed by the beauty of the landscape."

—Amelie

"With my mom, watching and listening to her play the piano, and my dad, it would have to be listening to him tell me all kinds of stories before I'd fall asleep at night. He's from Iran, so he always had interesting ghost and mystery stories."

—Irene

"My favorite memory of my parents from growing up are all the little 'flirty' moments I saw between them. I felt very loved and secure knowing my parents loved each other that much."

—JoyfulTxGal

Courtesy of the author

This is one of my favorite pictures of my dad and me from when I was a kid.

A s you know by now, my dad's behavior was always a little wacky. He could get totally lost going someplace he'd been a million times before. Post-it notes filled his walls. He would forget where he parked his car or lose his keys on a regular basis. I remember once he even forgot me in the car. I was about five, and we were in Iowa for one of our summer trips to see his family. I vividly recall being in a restaurant when the loudspeakers started blasting storm warnings. The staff rushed everyone out and people scattered as fast as they could. We jumped in the car and pulled up to the cabin just as the tornado hit. My father got out and ran into the house for shelter. The problem was that I was still in the car, which had begun spinning around in circles. I was in the backseat pounding on the glass, and it was only once my dad was safely inside with our family that he realized he had forgotten to bring me inside, too.

It took years to realize that he was suffering from the very early stages of Alzheimer's. As a family we wanted to care for him at home, but we couldn't keep him safe. He would wander off at all hours of the day and night and call us from pay phones in the middle of nowhere, with no idea where he was. Once my mom got a call from the police because they'd found my dad, completely disoriented, on a street corner. The only way they'd known who to call was that he was carrying my mom's purse. After years of struggling with this disease, eventually we had to move him into an assisted living facility, and it was heartbreaking.

My dad and I had always had a complicated relationship. He'd been unconventional and not always reliable, but in so many other ways he'd been a huge inspiration to me. He had lived such a colorful life, and I wanted to make some kind of record of all he'd done—while he still had the memories. For years he'd talked about going back to Iowa again to see his family, and I decided I wanted to give him one last chance to do that—for him, but also for me. I saw his illness progressing so rapidly, and I knew this was my last chance to go with my dad on one more adventure.

For as long as I can remember, I've carried a video camera with me wherever I went. Something about that lens has always felt safe and protective to me. We decided to drive across country to see his family in Iowa and Tennessee, and to visit the most important places from my father's history—and we decided to document it on film, so that my dad's memories would live on forever.

I was terrified about this trip, but I knew this was something I had to do. I had a few friends who said they would join us to support me on the journey, so we all set off to see America in a whole new way as father and daughter. Riding across country in an RV with my dad was one of the most intense experiences of my life, and there were times I wasn't sure we'd make it. My dad had become like a child in many ways—a big, strong child. Other times he seemed to forget that I wasn't a child anymore. On the few nights we stayed in motels, I'd have to write him a note to tell him where I was, just in case he woke up and couldn't remember. Even with the notes he'd have full-blown panic attacks if he was alone. It was as if he thought I was still a little girl, and he was afraid he'd lost me, or left me in the car again.

I will never forget when we arrived in Gadsden, Alabama, where my father had fought for civil rights in the 1960s. He was a true voice of change, fighting for equality for all. So many people don't know that some of our favorite actors from the sixties were not only incredible on-screen but were also profound humanitarians. I am so proud that my father was among them, using the power of media to create social change. He, Marlon Brando, Paul Newman, and Tony Franciosa had gone to Gadsden as ambassadors of goodwill. Now here we were so many years later. We were staying in a tiny little motel, and the locals had put up a sign in front of the building: WELCOME BACK, VIRGIL FRYE. Suddenly my dad had a total meltdown. His mind had gone right back to the sixties, and he was sure this welcome sign was actually a menacing threat that people were out to get him, and they were going to kill him.

The crisis passed, and one of the most moving moments of the trip for me was finding an amazing man who was just a little boy when my dad spoke in Gadsden. He remembered being in the church where my dad had been and how inspired he was by what my dad had said all those years ago. A survivor of some of the worst oppression the South had seen, this man was now a powerful elected official who took the time to thank my father for his contribution. It was a truly incredible moment.

When my dad and I started out on that journey, I thought I was doing the film to document my dad's life. Very quickly I realized that the film I was making was the story of our life together, and a last chance for us to get to know each other before it was too late. For all the difficult times I'd had with my dad over the years, what I remembered most, and what was truly most important, was the joy he brought to me.

When I got back from the trip and watched the footage, it also occurred to me that this film wasn't just for my family— it could possibly help a lot more people. I was not alone in this struggle of having a loved one suffer from Alzheimer's. I decided that I needed to share it with others. A truly amazing woman and editor, Yana Gorskaya, and I spent days and nights cutting together the footage into a documentary called *Sonny Boy* (the title was inspired by my father's boxing name, Sonny). It went on to win awards and play at numerous film festivals, but most important, I was able to touch the lives of others facing Alzheimer's and finally gain the courage to share my journey with my dad. So often with Alzheimer's disease it is a quiet tragedy that people are scared to talk about. It can tear families apart, but it can also bring them together. I am so truly grateful for the support that others affected by the disease have shared with me and for the Alzheimer's Association and their tireless work to find a cure. The face of Alzheimer's has changed. It is not something that affects only the elderly. It is something that touches all of us. And it truly is the long good-bye.

My father's disease has worsened in the years since our incredible road trip. He's been ill for my girls' entire lives, and we've talked about how their grandfather's mind is kind of a gray space, and what that means. Poet just asked me the other night as I was lying beside her putting her to sleep if my daddy would be sick forever. A tear fell from my eyes as I was caught off guard, emotions filling my heart. I said that even though he is sick now, he wasn't always that way and that he lived an amazing life. I told her that I believed he was in a magical place somewhere between two worlds, the physical one and the next one, but that I hoped he was happy wherever he was. And with that she smiled and went to sleep. It is incredible how much our children are aware of everything around them.

In March, I was invited by the Alzheimer's Association to join them in advocating on Capitol Hill for Alzheimer's research. We decided to make it a family affair, and I brought along Jason and the girls, my brother Meeno, his wonderful wife, and their daughters so that we could all experience it together. There we stood on the steps of the Lincoln Memorial, where my dad had marched with Martin Luther King, Jr., and we talked about what an incredible thing my children's grandfather had done along with so many others who fought for civil rights. As a family we remembered, for all of those who can no longer remember for themselves.

Here we are in front of the White House on our trip to Washington, D.C.

*   *   *

S.P.S.

What Alzheimer's has taught me . . .

The one thing I have come to realize more than anything else through the process of having a loved one with Alzheimer's is that as heartbreaking as it is, they live in the moment. Without memory of the past or able to look into the future, all they have is the here and now. I have learned from my father how to cherish what is in front of me, to hold on to the moment and love it, for we don't know what will come tomorrow.

What are the early signs?

For us it started with the small things. He would write down little reminders everywhere, forget to get gasoline for his car, etc. We did not realize that he was covering up just how little he could remember. He was a great actor, and he hid the progression of his disease. We would always make light of it, unaware of just how serious it had become. Certainly there are times we can all be forgetful, but if you are truly concerned for a loved one or yourself and you have any questions at all, the Alzheimer's Association is an amazing support. Remember that no matter what, you always must keep a sense of humor. That has been one of the greatest lessons for me. Otherwise it gets so heavy that you just want to cry. Better to laugh and cry than to be heartbroken and cry without the laughter.

Thank you . . .

I want to thank all of the social workers and caregivers who have shown my father such love as his symptoms have progressed. I also wish to reach out to all of the millions of families who are affected by Alzheimer's and dementia—thank you for sharing your stories, voices, and memories.

If you would like to learn more about how you can help the fight against Alzheimer's, please go to www.actionalz.org.

36

. . . .

Don't Stop Make-believing

Question of the day: What activity do you love doing with
your kids most?

"My daughter is only 15 months, so we haven't had tons of
experiences yet—but I just love bringing her out to do new
things. Seeing her react to just being out among people,
and all the new things she sees/hears/touches—it's exciting. Right now, our absolute favorite thing to do is dance!"

—Amanda

"I love to read to my kids and do adult size puzzles with
them, they love to help me, but it's great quality time for
everyone and no one gets into any fights!!!!"

—Irene

"Talking. I have a 21 year old son and a 13 year old daughter and they both talk to me often, sometimes about things
I don't want to know, but I listen with an open mind."

—Joseph

"Laughing, dancing, going to the beach, swimming, but mostly LAUGHING!!!!!"

—Natalie

"Arts and crafts."

—Dana

grew up on back lots of studios, and just the smell of a soundstage can send me into a nostalgic dream state. When I was really little, my mom had meetings at all the studios for her catering business, and she'd take me along with her everywhere she went. And of course I was glued to her side when she took Meeno to the sets where he was working—I especially remember his time on *Voyagers*, and his incredibly handsome and sweet costar, Jon-Erik Hexum.

Some of my earliest memories are of tape marks and hot lights, the big blue sky on the Paramount lot, and the massive false front of New York Street on the Universal lot (for the longest time I thought that all buildings had fronts with no backs). I remember the big old cafeterias, the trams going by—all those movie magic moments are ingrained in my DNA.

Hollywood was a game of pretend on a massive, fantastic scale, and I loved make-believe. I knew that the actors on-set were working—but to me it was all play. My childhood was all about seeing the world as a bright place, full of possibility.

My life at home was also full of magical moments. I remember when I was a baby, not even walking yet, and my mother woke up me and my brother in the middle of the night and took us out onto our little deck because it was hailing outside. I remember my dad dancing me to sleep to Leonard

Cohen songs. And I remember playing around the pool at my godparents' house—the amazing smell of wet cement, and all of us kids having the time of our lives with nothing but each other for entertainment. Now, that was magic.

I want my own girls' childhoods to be just as full of wonder. I'd be happy if they believed in Santa Claus forever. I hope they do. I mean, even I believe in Santa somewhere inside. For Jagger's last birthday, when the Mickey Mouse character came over, Poet noticed that there was a person inside. I swear I broke out in hives just imagining the floodgates of logic that were about to open up. If she learned that Mickey Mouse didn't exist, then what about the tooth fairy? And if the tooth fairy isn't real, then oh my God, what's next? I had to stop that right away—I think I said something about Mickey Mouse being so popular that he needed a little help.

When I'm playing with my girls, I'm still that little kid who loved magic and make-believe. Of course, it's hard sometimes to turn off the inner voices. But when I'm playing with them, I try to be in the moment. Sometimes there's nothing better for shutting off your brain than an eighties dance party. And I think it counts as exercise, too! (I do believe, I do believe.)

We invent lands and imagine them with mountains, rivers, and castles. On Earth Day we planted a strawberry garden and herbs that the girls could cook with. We love turning trash to treasure—we take old shoe boxes and paint them. We cover them with sparkles and glitter. I've come to realize that so much of what we can do with our kids doesn't cost any money. I can totally lose myself in coloring and playing dress-up with my girls.

I'll never forget the day I picked up Poet from school, and as we were driving home, there was a snowy shower in LA—it was a hailstorm. I suddenly remembered that hailstorm way back when I was a baby. I could still feel the cold pellets of that first hailstorm as they hit my face, and the way the cold felt under my little hands and feet. And here I was, enjoying the magic all over again with my daughter. It all comes full circle.

* * *

S.P.S.

Playing make-believe . . .

I love to transform our home into a princess palace, a barbershop, a camping trip, or a dance party. We get totally into it. Sometimes we get decked out as eighties prom queens, and other times we put on the stereo and just dance, dance, dance. It is great to see them being so free and for them to see that I can let go and have fun. Just tonight my girls said, "Mommy, come here." I walked into the living room and they had turned it into their very own Manhattan apartment. They had taken pillows and put them all around with a stereo and some of their other favorite toys. We listened to music and sang to each other. It was awesome. Sometimes we need to step out of ourselves as adults and remember the children we once were, and it is there where we can find the heart of our inner child. So get that dance party going, dress up in your eighties best, and dance like crazy. The more wacky and outrageous, the more fun you will all have.

A little sentence to finish . . .

When I was a kid, I used to make believe that I . . .

"Was on the TV show *Kids Incorporated*. My sisters and I used to act out each episode and sing the songs after we watched it."

—Sheila

"Was Barbie's manager and send her to autograph signings."

—Mikala

"Was a detective searching for clues of a suspect in my front and backyard."

—Collette

"Was Joey Lawrence (*Gimme a Break*, not *Blossom*) . . . and I'm a girl. Lol"

—Dana

"Was a Veterinarian and would take care of all my toy animals, as well as my real ones."

—Nicole A.G.

"Lived in a fort—we actually had a playroom that could easily be transformed, and was often a mass of tented-up blankets that we played in."

—Cari

37

· · · · · · · · · · · ·

Growing Pains

Question of the day: What do you consider to be your best parenting moment?

"When I can cater to both girls at the same time and they are both happy and content . . . spread my time evenly at the same time."

—Amy B.

"My little girl took stickers out of a book at a store and I had to explain to her that it was stealing since the book wasn't ours. I bought the book but told her she could not have it, she could earn it by doing little 'chores' like picking up her dirty clothes. The woman working at the store said I handled it so well, that so many others would have turned the other cheek and left. I wanted my daughter to understand and I believe it is something that has stayed with her."

—Amy L.

"It hasn't happened often but on really bad days I have my son write the specific date on a piece of paper, wad it up and throw it away. With the explanation that bad days happen, we don't have to dwell on it and tomorrow will be better. We don't have to think about it anymore."

—Sherry

"I honestly hope that I haven't had my best parenting moment yet, because my little one is still so small. If I had to pick one for now though, it would be when Joseph said to me, 'You're a good Mommy, Mommy.' He is the only critic that I need to worry about."

—Nicole A.G.

Sometimes we all feel a little lost. We ask ourselves if the path we are heading on is the right one. We question our choices and hope that everything will work out.

I remember when I was about twelve I got in an argument with my mom. I couldn't tell you now what it was about, but I said that I would go and live with my dad. I packed a little bag and went to my dad's, which lasted about twenty-four hours before I realized how much I missed home—the home my mom had built for us, the embrace of her warmth and love. Over the past year I felt a shift as a parent. I felt like I was getting deeper and deeper into the depths of parenthood. No one would ever say that being a parent is easy. But doesn't it seem like it should get a little easier as our kids get older? For me, not so much.

Over the past year, I've discovered that I'm going through my own growing pains as a parent. As my kids evolve from babies to toddlers to bigger kids, I have to grow right along with them. They need me more than ever before, and I am seeing in powerful ways how my behavior really affects theirs. I've seen how those times when I'm distracted can really result in them acting out. They need us so much, and yet sometimes Mom and Dad just want to curl up and have a few moments to catch their own breath.

Of course, it's totally healthy and necessary to take breaks, and no one can possibly be a perfect superparent all the time. We do the best that we can, but sometimes it can be hard, and that's okay.

Watching my kids grow into thoughtful, interesting people has taught me what the heart of parenting really is. It's much bigger, deeper, and more challenging than changing diapers and showering them with hugs and kisses. As our kids get more complicated, we need to become even more thoughtful as parents, and we have to figure out new ways to communicate with them.

Our kids are these little sponges soaking up their world, and we need to keep helping them understand it—even if we don't have all the answers. They have all these big emotions and new experiences to navigate—sibling dynamics, school, and first conflicts with friends. It's not enough to tell an upset child that everything will be okay. They need more than that from us. Just recently, Poet was really upset about some trouble she was having with a friend. It seemed like the end of the world to her. After listening to what was going on, I told her that when I was her age, I'd had conflicts with my friends, too, and that Tori and I used to get in fights all of the time. She looked at me with big, round eyes, and said, "You did?" And then I pointed out to Poet that Tori and I worked through all those conflicts and now we're still best friends, thirty years later. That made such a huge difference to Poet. Our kids can feel like they are totally alone in the experiences they are having, and it's so powerful for them to feel your compassion and realize that they're not the only person in the universe who has ever had whatever problem they're going through. Like us, as kids peel away the onion, the layers to who they are get deeper and reveal more to us each and every day.

It's awe-inspiring what a huge impact we have as parents. Our children's behavior is truly shaped by the experiences, attention, and nurturing that we give them. They grow up so fast, and the events of an afternoon spent reading with them, or running on a beach, or playing ball in the park can have an incredibly lasting effect. What an amazing gift that is to us as parents, and what a huge responsibility to live up to. But I really believe that everything we put into our children feeds their little roots and helps them grow into the big kids, tweens, and young adults that they'll be before we know it. And then one day we can stand back and see what amazing people we brought into this world.

* * *

S.P.S.

When our kids need a little extra . . .

When our kids are upset about something, they don't always have the words to tell us what's wrong. Sometimes (often) they let actions speak louder than words . . . meaning, they act out. The girls and I recently made a deal that when they feel like they need some extra attention, rather than act out, all they have to do is come tell me that they need a little one-on-one time. I've also learned to be more attentive to the signs they are giving me, because I know that I have just as much to learn from them as they do from me.

A note from the heart . . .

I really believe that it's the quality of the time that we spend with our kids that makes all the difference in the world. The evolution of these minds is so inspired by how we connect with each other. I speak this from my heart, because this is a journey I am on, just like you, and I am a work in progress— we all are, but I really believe that we must get on the floor and play, dance our hearts out, share, and be present.

38

. . . .

To All You Dads out There

Question of the day: What do you think is the best part of being a dad?

"I think the best part of being a Dad, especially for stay-at-home mom situations, would have to be that when they come in the door . . . it's a celebration every time!"

—Nicole A.G.

"As a mom, I think the best part of being a dad is getting all the fun stuff while mom deals with all the icky stuff. Lol. I know, I know, not all dads avoid dirty diapers and booger noses like the plague."

—Dana

"I'm not a dad, but I know that my dad loved it when we reminded him that he was our protector—bad storms, any kind of calamity, and he was the one we all turned to. He had broad shoulders, and was always making us feel safe and protected."

—Cari

"While most parents today serve a few jobs to get by and my family is no different there is a great sense of pride and accomplishment to contribute as a provider to my family. The balance between the job and spending quality time with my family is always at odds and when we are in the moment as a family there is no better feeling. It really gives a sense of what matters most."

—Jason G.

Soleil

Jason and the girls on the beach in Hawaii

The other day, I was in the grocery store and I saw a dad there with his baby in a carrier, and I thought, *Oh my God, how great! What a good dad!* I wanted to go up and pat him on the shoulder. Then I stopped myself and I thought, *Wait a second. Why would I want to congratulate a dad on taking his kid to the grocery store? Would I ever do that to a mom? Never!*

To tell the truth, it didn't even occur to me to do a special chapter in this book for dads, because I thought of the whole book as being for all parents. I mean, sure, there is some particularly mom-centric stuff in here (see: granny panties and/or vagina spray), but I really think of all of us parents as being on this journey together. And I have a husband who is totally involved in our kids' lives, and I wouldn't want it any other way.

So I was really surprised when one day, my totally involved husband said, "You're doing a chapter for dads, right?" I told him that the whole book was for dads as well as moms. He shook his head. "You gotta do a chapter for dads." He felt really strongly about it.

And I think I know why. It's for the same reason that I wanted to congratulate that dad in the grocery store. We moms often *say* that we want dads to be just as involved as moms, but then sometimes we treat them like they're—well, less important. Sometimes we even treat them like they don't know what they're doing. I've heard so many dads complain about being out with their babies and having total strangers (always women) come up to them to give them advice or tell them that they're doing something wrong. As much unwanted advice as moms can get, dads get way more. And how many times have you heard someone say that a dad was home "babysitting" his kids? Do we ever say that a mom is babysitting her kids? Of course not!

All those things we think and say can send the message that dads aren't really included in this parenting thing—at least not to the same degree that moms are. We say that we want parenting to be fifty-fifty, but how often do we try to control how our partners do things or hover over them when they're doing their part? And how often do we even roll our eyes when we think they're not doing things the right way (meaning: our way)?

I like to think that I've never rolled my eyes at Jason (at least not to his face), but I know that I've been guilty of grabbing more than my fifty percent share of parenting. Maybe I have a lot going on one day, and he offers to pick up the girls from school. Instead of gratefully accepting his help, I say, "No, no, I'll do it; I've got it covered." Partly I think it's because, as moms, we feel guilty if we don't do everything for our kids, or that maybe we'll miss something important if we're not always there.

But of course, that's not doing us or our kids any favors. Single parenting is incredibly tough, and if we're lucky enough to have a partner to co-parent with us, why wouldn't we want to take full advantage? It makes us stronger as a couple when we're on the same page, and it gives our kids an incredibly important message that men are just as capable of being loving and nurturing as women are. And that's definitely the kind of world we want for our kids.

* * *

S.P.S.

. . . .

Speak up . . .

From the time our babies are newborns, especially if the mom is breastfeeding and taking a maternity leave, moms can get it in their heads that their kids need them to do everything. Somehow it feels wrong not to take care of every single need that our children have. Soon it becomes second nature, and that pattern just keeps repeating itself even as our babies grow into bigger kids. Dads can get kind of used to it, too. If Mom has always been the one to go to the pediatrician's appointment, it might not occur to Dad to take time off from work and be the one to go instead of Mom. It's never too late to break that pattern, though. Sometimes it's as simple as speaking up. So to all you dads out there, if you want to be more involved, say so. And you moms out there, if you want your partner to be more involved, speak up. You might be surprised how happy your partner is to take on their fair share.

39

. . . .

Mix Tape

Question of the day: If you were going to make a mix tape of your life, what would your theme songs be?

"Everything . . . life has been one jumbled mess . . . but I wouldn't trade it for the world!"

—Nicole P.

"'Keep the Car Running'—Arcade Fire . . . 'Over My Head'—The Fray . . . 'Divine Romance'—Phil Wickam . . . 'Angel'—Jimi Hendrix . . . 'Cry Baby'—Janis Joplin."

—Collette

"Love Guns N' Roses, John Williams, Jerry Goldsmith, James Horner and Roxette. I listen to music nearly constantly. I'm thinking I would have a 16 volume CD set!"

—Allen

"'Don't Worry, Be Happy' :) 'I Hope You Dance,' and most of all: 'God Bless the Broken Road.'"

—Cari

I f I had to come up with the soundtrack for my life, this
would be it. Or at least a really good start. I love that the
songs I sang in the car when I was eight are the same songs
I'm singing with my little girls today. It was so much fun
putting this list together, and I didn't want to stop. You'll
see musicians and whole albums as well because sometimes
I couldn't pick just one song. I could keep going and going,
so consider this a partial list that is to be continued.

Putting this list together made me think how great it
would be if we all made mix tapes for our kids on a regular
basis—little musical autobiographies of ourselves to show
them how we traveled the same path that they're just beginning. So, here's my mix tape . . . what's yours?

Courtesy of the author

Here I am listening to music as a little girl. I miss cassette tapes and
making mixes on them. Let's bring it back!

"Don't Stop Believin'" (Journey)

Picture me, ten years old, riding with Tori in the backseat of Rick Schroder's white Porsche. He was starring in *Silver Spoons*, and we'd all been at an event at Magic Mountain. My mom said it was okay for him to give us a ride to the restaurant where we were going for dinner. Rick blasted Journey on the stereo and drove as fast as he could, and Tori and I were in heaven. Now whenever this song comes on the radio, my girls say, "It's Mommy's song!"

"Here Comes My Girl" (Tom Petty and the Heartbreakers)

Tom Petty always reminds me of the phase in my life when I was running around with Danny O'Connor (House of Pain). We would spend nights cruising around the city while I filmed everything on my video camera. One night in particular I found myself getting a tattoo on Sunset Boulevard while Tom Petty was playing in the background. I felt like I was in a music video.

"Eternal Flame" (The Bangles)

Sigh. This brings back such sweet memories of summer camp in the 1980s, sitting around the bonfire, talking about life and love.

"Cool Rider" (*Grease 2* soundtrack)

Best. Song. Ever. I'm pretty convinced of this. Tori and I danced through the aisles to this song when *Grease 2* came out, and I've sung "Cool Rider" probably every week since. Now my two *Grease*-obsessed girls do the same thing.

There's nothing like seeing a five-year-old and a two-year-old singing "I want a c-o-o-o-o-l r-i-d-e-r."

Billie Holiday (just pick a song, I love them all)
When I hear her voice, it reminds me so much of my teenage years. I would listen to her in the rain by myself and really feel my teen-angst blues when I had them.

"Crash into Me" (Dave Matthews Band)
This was our wedding song, and I still love it so much. It is also a classic example of a song with lyrics that seem a lot racier when grandparents are sitting in the room.

"Leaving on a Jet Plane" (John Denver)
We always sang this song at camp, and now I sing it to the girls almost every night. But my most vivid memory of this song is when I was eight and I went to Puerto Rico with my mom, Meeno, and Tori to do a personal appearance. When we arrived, we found out that the organizers had thought that I was a singer as well as an actress. So my brother managed to bang out a few chords on a guitar, while Tori and I sang "Leaving on a Jet Plane" complete with choreography—in front of sixty thousand people. We reassured ourselves that no one we knew would ever see it. Then it was broadcast all over Telemundo. This was my one and only brush with being an actress-singer.

"La Di Da Di" (Slick Rick and Dougie Fresh)
When we did the *Andy Williams Christmas Special* in Finland in the eighties, Alphonso Ribeiro and Malcolm-Jamal Warner played this song over and over and over again. It's

still completely hilarious to me that my lasting musical memory of a trip with Andy Williams is a hip-hop song.

"Pink Moon" (Nick Drake)

This song reminds me so much of my cross-country trip with my dad, when we listened to it every day. It moves me so much.

"F* and Run" (Liz Phair)**

I picked just one song, but honestly Liz Phair's *Exile in Guyville* got me through my teenage years. I think we all have an album like that.

"Mr. Tambourine Man" (Bob Dylan)

This song reminds me so much of my godfather, Joseph. I love and miss him every day.

"Maggie May" (Rod Stewart)

Ever since I was really little, my brother would play this song on his guitar for me when I couldn't fall asleep. Even when I was a teenager and visiting him at college, he'd pull out his guitar and play it for me. That's love.

"We Don't Have to Take Our Clothes Off" (Jermaine Stewart)

Imagine me and Joey Lawrence dancing to this song at Disneyland, both of us about nine years old. So funny.

"Golden Years" (David Bowie)

I put this song on the video I made for Jason's and my tenth wedding anniversary, intercut with so many memories from our life together. I could watch it over and over.

"Holiday" (Madonna)

This is one of my favorite Madonna songs. It was one of the first cassette tapes I ever owned, and I wore it out. Now my girls love it, too. What's not to love?

"The Tide Is High" (Blondie)

When I was eight, I had this very sophisticated friend who looked just like a young Madonna. She introduced me to Blondie's music, and this song still makes me remember those days when you couldn't get cooler than Debbie Harry.

"If You Were Here" (Thompson Twins)

Aw, that scene in *Sixteen Candles*. Oh how it melts my heart even still. Jake leaning in for the kiss over the cake. This has since become a song I love to share with my husband.

"Summer Nights" (*Grease* soundtrack)

Simply one of my all-time favorite songs to sing with my girls. It always takes me back to my childhood.

***Beautiful Girls* soundtrack**

This reminds me of my husband, when we fell in love, and every moment in between.

Eek-A-Mouse

This music brings back to me my time living in New York, Justin Pierce, Harold, my amazing friend firefighter Pete—one of the greatest guys I know—and being young and crazy, running around town with skateboarders and artists.

Jeff Buckley

His album *Grace* really got me through some crazy times. When I finished my documentary about my dad, *Sonny Boy*, I had the incredible chance to share it with Jeff's mother. We sat in her apartment and watched it side by side, and it was a truly moving experience.

Tori Amos

My awesome roommate Matt and I would listen to *Little Earthquakes* over and over in our one-bedroom apartment in New York City in the 1990s. I loved those days.

Norah Jones

I must have listened to *Come Away with Me* a thousand times, and every song strikes a chord. I'll never forget when Jason and I saw her in concert in New York City with Demi and Ashton. Norah and I had a bonding experience backstage.

Jenny Lewis

Jenny was one of my childhood friends. We traveled together and we would sing songs as little kids. She always had an amazing voice. She is now one of the most talented, unbelievable female singers around.

"Tainted Love" (Soft Cell)

This always brings me back to Alfie's Soda Pop Club, all of the faces, and all of the dancing, laughter, and fun.

Let Love Rule (Lenny Kravitz)

One of the greatest albums ever made. My brother and I have seen Lenny in concert about ten times.

Elliott Smith

His voice is the background music for so much of my adult life. One of the greatest!

Aimee Mann

Her music really reminds me of finishing the documentary about my father. Her music inspired me.

Tracy Chapman (Tracy Chapman)

I was around eleven when this album came out, and I listened to it over and over again. I would write in my journal for hours late at night, reflecting on life, love, and all of the questions you have at that age.

"Sometimes It Snows in April" (Prince)

I've listened to this song a thousand times, and I love every lyric. Simply one of the greatest songs ever.

* * *

S.P.S.

Now it's your turn . . .

Write down your favorite songs and take a little time to remember each one. Ah, the nostalgia. Then make that mix for a friend, a spouse, or a partner, and share it with them. Do the same for your kids and tell them stories about why you love each and every song.

40

. . . .

Press Pause

Question of the day: How do you try to savor the special moments with your kids?

"I'm a picture fiend. I take pictures all the time. I also write . . . I've got tons of journals filled with crazy stuff they do. They are my inspiration to write."

—AnaLiesa

"With teary eyes, lots of pictures, and the knowledge that they are only getting better with age."

—Allen

"By fully realizing that they grow up way too fast and you'll miss these moments when they're gone. Don't get too busy that you miss the little moments, too. I think of those moments when I am stressed and tired. It helps me to put things in perspective."

—Jennifer

"I am a sentimental memento crazy person! I take pictures and videos like crazy, I also save special projects my kids do and give to me. I keep a journal by my bed, and every night before I go to sleep, I write a little bit in it about their day and cool things they did or funny stories that happened or accomplishments or new things they learned that day. Helps me to reminisce."

—Whitney

Not that long ago I brought home a copy of one of my favorite books, Shel Silverstein's *The Giving Tree*, for my girls. I couldn't wait to read it to them, because I loved that book so much when I was a kid. Maybe I'd forgotten how sad it was, or maybe I was reading it through new eyes, but it knocked me out. I cried, and cried, and cried the first time I read it to Poet and Jagger. Then, just at the moment I finished the last page, I had this amazing memory from preschool. I remembered how my teacher told us that there was a secret design hidden inside an apple, and she had us guess what it was. Then she showed us how, if you cut the apple a certain way, you would find a beautiful star inside.

So I wiped my tears, I closed *The Giving Tree*, and I said, "Hey girls, do you want to see something really exciting?" Then, just as my teacher had done, I had the girls guess what the hidden design inside an apple would be. A heart? No . . . A triangle? No . . . Then finally, I cut the apple that special way, and there was the star inside. It was so beautiful, and their eyes opened up in awe. It was a good mommy moment.

If I've learned anything as a mom, it's that our lives are made up of special moments. And if there is one piece of advice that I'd give any parent, no matter how young or old their children are, it would be to take more pauses and appreciate all those little moments. Each one is such a gift. Because we can't possibly give one hundred percent all the time—but we can give one hundred percent to a moment. And we can feel really good about that.

In the last year, I've been focused on taking more pauses just to savor those little moments—when the girls are dancing with their dad, or we're all driving in the car singing. Not every hour of our lives together is going to be great, and at the end of any given day I might feel guilty for all the ways I was imperfect. But I also know that if I've taken those pauses, then hopefully I've also filled my girls with the kind of colorful, rich moments that create lifelong memories.

Just recently I listened to a talk by the dean of a grammar school who also happens to be a philosopher. He said that at his school, they have a "generation day" every year, and each year he notices the same thing—the parents are rushing their kids, moving them on to the next activity. Faster, faster, go, go. All the while the grandparents are telling their grandchildren to slow down and enjoy the moment.

The really amazing thing is that if we could actually hit the pause button once in a while and see the world through our kids' eyes, we'd find that we have just as much to learn from them as they have to learn from us. As parents we never stop learning—from our own parents, our friends, and yes, our children. I'm still learning patience and how to communicate with my kids, and I'm still making mistakes all the time. It's not as if just because we're grown-ups and responsible, now all of a sudden we have all the answers. I know I don't.

So when I'm confused, unsure, and wondering if I have this parenting thing down at all, I close my eyes and I remember the little girl inside me—the girl who couldn't stop asking why. Sometimes I raise my hand and ask for advice, and other times I do my own soul searching. On the days that I fall down or have those not-so-perfect parenting moments, I tell myself that it is all going to be okay and I will do better tomorrow. It is in the times when we feel most broken that we can discover how to be better parents, and it is in the pauses and dashes in between when we are able to fill life with all of the delicious discoveries, images, and snapshots that we will carry with us throughout our lifetimes.

* * *

S.P.S.

Make a star . . .

Here's how to cut an apple and find the secret star inside: Take your apple and set it on the table. Instead of cutting it up and down like you would usually do, lay it on its side and cut it though the center. It should be cut into two circles. Now open it, and there it is, that magical little star.

Everything else sometimes has to wait . . .

Just as I was writing the last pages of this book, my girls were running around the house and I went to ask my mom a question. At that moment, I heard a loud crash and ran into the living room to find my two-year-old lying behind the couch with shattered glass all around. I picked her up and blood was running down the back of her neck. My heart was pounding, I was so scared. Poet stood by me as I rushed to call 911. My little baby had a two-and-a-half-inch open gash in the back of her head. I called that very same doctor who had taken care of Poet and found myself in the doctor's office pacing with my child in my arms, a total wreck, just like all of the other mothers in the world who have gone through these moments before me. My deadline would have to wait. Everything would have to wait, because all that mattered was being present for my babies. So again we must remember to take the pauses, because if we don't do it for ourselves, then someone bigger will do it for us.

Make a moment . . .

Make a list of the special moments that you most treasure from your time as a parent. Use that for your inspiration and revisit it often. Now make a little sign and put it anywhere that you spend time—the mirror, the fridge, the pantry, the car—that says, "Never forget to pause for the moments in between," and let it remind you even in the midst of chaos (our own happy chaos) to take the time to savor a moment and create a memory that will live on long after our dash.

Here's a moment of us running on the beach that my brother captured. It's in times like this that I really feel like pressing pause.

Acknowledgments

I am so truly grateful for all of the love and support that I have received throughout this process. There are so many people who have helped me make the dream of sharing my Happy Chaos a reality, and I am eternally thankful for the time and love put into this process.

First and foremost, I want to thank everyone who contributed by sending in their stories and sharing their moments with me. To all of the moms, dads, friends, and grandparents who made me feel not so alone as a messy parent doing her best to find the balance in life, you inspire me everyday. To my family who fills my world with love and support each and everyday, I love you.

My incredible editor, Carrie Thornton, you believed in this book since the very beginning; you have been a true champion for me, my vision, and have supported me throughout this process. I am so grateful to you for diving into this incredible adventure and for your honesty and encouragement throughout. I am so lucky to have you as an editor and friend. You are amazing and really understand this beautiful and often messy adventure in parenting.

To my husband who gives me so much love and support, who read page after page, and who always encouraged me to share our Happy Chaos. You are the most incredible husband, teammate, father, and best friend, and this journey of life is one that I am forever thankful to be sharing with you.

Poet and Jagger, you are my inspiration, my little goddesses, my loves, my life. Mama loves you with every part of her heart and soul. I learn more from you than you could ever learn from me. You are the greatest teachers and children a mom could ever dream of, and I love you for eternity.

Mom, you are the roots of my heart and soul. You gave me endless love growing up and taught me to be a dreamer. You supported every creative bone in my body and showed me that even when I fell, I could find my feet again. You filled our home with all of the love and inspiration imaginable for your kids and made our home a safe haven for all. I am forever thankful for you showing me the way, while allowing me to be my own person. You taught me all about mothering by being the best mother. The dancing in the rain, the sleeping outside under the stars, the stories you would tell—you imprinted all of the best memories into my heart, mind, and soul. I love you. Shawn, thank you for being another dad to us all and for your continued love. You are truly a big teddy bear and a wonderful grandfather, and I am forever grateful to have you in our lives.

Meeno and Ilse, you bring such adventure and love to our lives. You are pillars of strength and wisdom and make us laugh throughout our days. You keep the cycle of life constantly abundant with riches of art, images of love, and constant beauty. Meeno, you capture it all with your lens the way only you know how with that magic eye, and I am so proud to be your little sis and to have the opportunity to work with you and your genius. You brought this cover to life!

Acknowledgments

Bindi and Mette, you are the little ladies who continue to inspire your auntie in all of your brilliant ways. You keep our house full of joy and bring music to our lives. I love you so very much.

Mema, my godmother and my amazing friend, thank you for every late-night talk and for every time you have been there on the other line ready to share stories. I turn to you always as I know that I am safe, heard, and understood in your embrace.

Bapu: I miss you now, I miss you yesterday, I miss you tomorrow, I miss you always, but I know you are watching and, just like you inspired in me, "I am enjoying the ride."

Daddy, whatever world your mind wonders in, I know you would be proud and I will forever carry on the legacy of your memory. I love you, Papa.

Tori, my best friend since age two. What can I say? Throughout every chapter of writing this book, I would have a flashback to you, to us, to our years growing up. There is no length of time during my life or a period in which there wasn't you. You have been there for me through and through. I love you beyond words.

Andy, I am so happy that you picked up the phone on that day. I will never forget when you said to me in your sweet New York accent, "Just write me a letter of the book you want to write." You made me feel so very comfortable from the very first moment we spoke. You have been such an incredible support. You have never swayed me away from being a hundred percent myself. From the moment I sent you my scrapbook-looking pitch and you totally got it, to keeping me sane throughout the process, even when I would call you on the verge of tears, your calm and guidance has been a true anchor for me. You are not only outstanding at what you do, you are my friend and I am so happy to have shared this journey with you. To the rest of WME, thank you for the support. To Brooke, Justin, and Tahira, you rock!

Jane, I love you so very much. Oh, how you believed in me and saw this way before anyone else did. Jane would call me on the phone every few months and say, "Soleil, when are you going to write a book?" I would say, "Soon, I know, I know. I need to do it." She would then say, "You need to meet my friend and agent, Andy." I would say, "Okay, sure." Then we would talk about other things, and about a month later she would call me and say, "Soleil, when are you going to write a book?" This went on for about a year, the very same conversation until finally one day I spoke to her incredible friend Andy and the rest was history. Jane, I would not be here today without your guidance, insight, and inspiration. You are so much more than a friend. You know how to foresee the future with that crystal ball of yours, and you encourage people to believe that they can accomplish anything. You make us all feel bigger and stronger just by having you in our lives, and I am forever grateful for those calls, and for you sitting on the line when I would get exhausted and say, "How am I going to finish this?" I loved that you simply said, "I'm sorry, now keep moving forward."

Lisa Rowe, you have been such an incredible friend to me. I have turned to you so many times throughout this process, and you listened to my endless calls at night, you gave me advice, and you were there for me each and every day. One of my favorite memories throughout the whole process was me and you sitting and looking through all of my photo albums to pick which pictures to include in the book. We laughed for hours. I love you from the bottom of my heart, and to your beautiful boys, Brad and Hopper, we are so grateful to have you as our extended family. Love you always.

Hillary: I am so grateful to you for so many things. From all of our moments before Poet's birth to yes, finding my placenta (I hope it was mine) to sitting by my side and listening to me read paragraphs out loud. The constant two A.M. e-mails I would send you with chapters asking for notes or help with the kids while I was writing. You have stepped up in every way imaginable. You are more than a friend. You are like a sister to me and I love you like crazy.

Peternelle van Arsdale, thank you so very much for listening to my stories and for being such a huge support throughout this process. I am thankful for the way in which you put up with all of my incomplete sentences and wacky ideas. I know it was an adventure, and I am very happy to have been on it with you. You helped me to bring our crazy chaotic world to life.

Jessica Horvath, thank you for your kindness and support. You have been so great to work with and I love your passion for this project. You have had such grace every step of the way. Your encouragement meant so much to me.

Brian Tart, thank you for believing in me and my Happy Chaos. I am so excited to be on this incredible adventure with you and your team.

Christine Ball, you are so fantastic and have had an incredible vision for this book. Thank you for being the voice on the other line that listened to my excitement and matched it with equal enthusiasm.

Thank you to Stephanie Hitchcock, Carrie Swetonic, and Ava Kavyani, for your time and commitment to this book, and to Julia Gilroy, Alissa Amell, and Monica Benalcazar—each and every one of you in the Dutton and Penguin family have made my dreams a reality.

* * *

Demi and Ashton, your love and inspiration mean the world to me. You build people up to be the best that they can possibly be and are two of the most giving, generous, and loving people I know. From birthing team, to advice, to just providing a good laugh or being the person I can to turn to, you are always there for me. I love you so much, and to your beautiful girls, Tallulah, Rumer, and Scout, thank you for showing us all of the joy and happy chaos we had to look forward to before we ever had our own kids. You are each a brilliant, beautiful, and insightful woman who I feel so lucky to get to watch grow.

Margie, Clyde, Larry, and Marilyn, thank you for raising such a terrific son. I love him with every bit of my heart and soul. You are wonderful grandparents and we are truly grateful to have your love and support in our lives. To Sean and Ashley, thanks for being such a great auntie and uncle. We love you.

Gina Bianchini, you have been a guiding force of light to me throughout the past few years. Your friendship and inspiration mean the world to me. You inspire me to want to help change the world to be a better place. You are not only one of the most brilliant minds I know, but you also don't mind sitting on the floor to map out the future, while being an amazing friend and leader. I love you so very much.

Maggie and Greg, I adore you. Maggie, your friendship

has been one of the closest of my life and you always encouraged me to believe in myself! You have been there for me throughout my many stages and I love you guys from the bottom of my heart.

Rebecca and Eric: You are two of the most incredible people we know and I am forever grateful for your friendship.

Ariana and Petro, I feel so blessed to have you both in our lives. You are true friends and we love you so much.

To Paige Tolmach and Matt Tolmach, thank you for everything. I am so happy that we have been on this journey together and am grateful that we were able to bring our little seed to life.

Firefighter Pete—my brother, my friend—I love you and all of our years in NYC. You continue to be a force in my life and you inspire me to believe in all of the magic. You remind me of who I am and who I will always be, and to Jaclyn, you always keep it real! Much love.

To Kimo and family, thank you for being both a big brother and extended family. I am grateful for the mountain of memories that we share together.

* * *

Randi Zuckerberg, my incredible friend and soul sister, thank you for your kindness and love.

Eric and Karyn Lammerding, your friendship has meant so much to me and I feel so very lucky for all of our moments together.

Josh, Jenny, and all of my friends at Target—thank you for believing in me. I am so proud and grateful to work with you.

Acknowledgments

Everyone at Deca, I am having so much fun doing our show. Thanks for the laughs and smiles.

Anna Babbitt and the whole team at New Wave, I am so excited for the adventure that we are on and the road ahead.

Jack Gray, you have been such a fantastic friend and told me that I could make it happen. There is no one who I love sharing a cab with more in NYC than you and I adore you.

Alyson Croft, you are a terrific friend who has always been there for me. I am forever grateful.

Robert Kelly, thank you for making my best friend so happy and for always being a sounding board for me.

Teddy Bass, you are not only the most incredible trainer in the world, you are a loyal friend and a constant inspiration.

Heather McComb: Thank you for always being such a special and beautiful part of my life.

Melissa Joan Hart, Paula, and the whole Hart family, thank you for all of your love and support over the years and for being a second family.

Keleigh Thomas, Arpi, and everyone at Sunshine Sachs, thank you for taking this project on and for sticking with me on this wild road.

Mike Lincoln, thank you for everything. You have been a force of ongoing encouragement.

Special thanks to David Altman, Barry Greenfield, and Ellen Nadel. Thank you for always keeping us on the right track.

Sarah, Ali, and your gorgeous kids, I love you.

* * *

To Arlene, Larry, and the whole Sommer family, Bonnie Bruckheimer, Miranda, Scott, Carol, Rio, Dakota, and the rest of the big extended family we have, thank you for the get-togethers, laughter, and joy you bring into our lives.

Iris, Constance, and the whole Walker family, I am so thankful for you being such an amazing family to all of us.

Floyd (Daddy 2), thank you for those wonderful pancakes and Sunday mornings. I will always hold them close to my heart.

To Gyorgie and the whole Peluce family, you inspire me so very much and have always welcomed me with open arms. Thank you.

Lauren, thank you for sitting by my side with a thousand photo albums and for taking notes while I talked about my crazy adventures. You came on to something that was in full swing and were ready to dive in and willing to help with anything. I am forever thankful.

Matt Boren: Oh my, I can't believe this is the part in the book where I get to thank you. Thank you for our years, our mixes, our poems, and our adventures. Thanks to your whole entire family for welcoming me as part of their own. It has been a roller coaster, an adventure, but the road will always bring me back to you. I love you, MB.

To Punky Brewster, a character who will forever live on in my heart. You are me and I am you! PUNKY POWER FOREVER!

To Brandon Tartikoff, I will miss you always and forever. You gave Punky her spirit and me my first big break at dreaming bigger than I ever imagined. You were television at its greatest, when being a part of a network was truly being a part of a family. As a kid there was no other place I would have rather been. I hope you are watching me from a giant cloud and that I have made you proud as I carry a piece of you with me. To Lilly and the whole Tartikoff family, thank you for your love throughout the years.

To David Duclon, your vision and creation will forever be so close to my heart. You made every day fun. We were kids first and foremost and there was no better playground than the set of *Punky*. To Gary Menteer and the entire staff of writers, producers, and crew. To anyone who ever gave me a piggyback ride down the halls, applied makeup with care, kept me fed and happy, or taught us that jumping off of furniture with pogo sticks was just as important as showing up to set. You each helped form the mother I am today and I carry your lessons with me always. To Gene Doucette and all of the team that gave Punky her unique style and inspired millions of people to carry on the legacy of mismatched shoes and individuality. To my friends in the cast: George Gaines, you were such a brilliant actor to work beside. I will forever remember your talent, your warmth, and your heart. To the fantastic actors and family that I got to play with on a daily basis: Cherrie, Amy, Casey, T. K. Carter, Susie, and the rest of the awesome cast. To the families of the cast and Mrs. Johnson, thank you for the sleepovers and great laughs throughout our days. Cherrie, I am forever grateful that you did not run away from me that first day we met and you saw my crazy drawings. Instead you became my friend and family.

To the Wright family, thank you for your kindness and for always opening your home and hearts to me. Thank you for allowing Maggie the freedom to make my childhood so much more colorful.

To Yana Gorskaya, you have been such an incredible friend to me. There is no one I would rather be locked in an editing room with than you. You are a brilliant storyteller and friend, and have guided me through some of my toughest moments. I love you and your family so very much. To Gina Leonard, who was the first person to jump on the *Sonny Boy* journey and who never stopped believing in me. Thank you for believing in me, and to Todd Hickey and the rest of the team on our adventure, I am so grateful that you gave me one of the greatest gifts, the ability to carry on my father's memory.

To my brother Sean, Aunt Carol, Uncle Mel, Uncle Junior, Nancy, and the rest of my Iowa and Tennessee family, I love you.

To Dan, Shervin, Kevin Rose, Ev, and my friends up North. Thank you for the continued inspiration.

Charles Porch, Erin Kanaley, Mandy Zibart, and all of my friends at Facebook—much love and thanks to you.

Terra Williger and Sally Mueller, you have both been such forces in my life. I am truly grateful.

Sean and the whole team at J/P/HRO, thank you for opening my eyes to the world in a whole new light.

To the Green family, I appreciate that you recognized, from the time that I was a child, my potential to turn into a somewhat normal adult.

My good friend Eric Buterbaugh, I love you and always will.

Jeff Ballard, you will always have a special place in my heart. Thank you for always reminding me of the child within.

To Marlon Brando, Paul Newman, Tony Francioso, and Dennis Hopper, thank you for touching my father's life and, in turn, leaving a legacy for me to share with my children and generations to come.

To Grandma Jackie, thank you for being an incredible god-grandmother to me, and to Evelyn who embraced me like I was her own. To both Roses, we carry you with us always.

Acknowledgments

To the grandparents who are watching over us now, thank you for paving the way for us.

To Carol and all of the Mastersons, thank you for always providing a second home for me and for pushing us to be messy and have fun as kids.

The Goss family: Shalon and Ed, watching you has taught me the power of human strength. To Bryten and Rose, thank you for encouraging me to live my dash in between to the fullest.

To Carol Bovill, and the rest of the Wilshire Boulevard Temple, thank you for your guidance and for always serving as a pillar of strength for us. To Rabbi Leder, there are some people you come across in your lifetime that leave an indelible mark on you, and for us, you are that person.

To all of my childhood crushes, and I know there were so many more, thank you for inspiring me and my love of boys from a very young age. This one goes out to Jake Ryan, R.J. Williams, Chad Allen, Danny Masterson, Brian Green, Andy Gibb, Johnny Depp, C. Thomas Howell, Charlie Sheen, Mark-Paul Gosselaar, Mario Lopez, Balthazar Getty, Mark Wahlberg, and Joey Lawrence.

The Weiss family, thank you for always being an extended family to me.

To Jonathan Brandis and the Brandis family, our friendship throughout the years was one of the closest. My teenage memories are filled with visits from you and a special appreciation for my cat suits. There is a chapter in my heart that is dedicated just to you and our teenage glory.

Justin Pierce, Harold, Rodney, E, and my incredible friends whose memory I hold with me each and everyday—I miss you always.

Acknowledgments

Taylor, Ashley, and the entire Little Seed team. Thank you beyond words.

To Kidada, Quincy, Rashida, and Peggy, for letting me have so many sleepovers, and to Rashida, who put up with us.

To Bonnie Bishop and Karen Francho, who embraced my quirks from an early age and taught me to always feel comfortable even if it meant showing up to school in only a t-shirt.

Thank you to all of the people mentioned in this book and to those friends who are a constant inspiration. I know someone will be left out, so I am truly sorry in advance.

* * *

A special thank you to: Dr. Robert Katz, Dr. Jay Gordon, Dr. Vicki Rappaport, Dr. Soram, Dr. Sugarman, and all of the Docs. Danny O'Connor, The House of Pain, Cathy Moriarty, Joey, and all of my friends from Mulberry Street Pizzeria. Thank you for being a highlight in my life. Kevin Connelly, Scott Caan, Marissa Ribisi, Chrissy Hudson, Danny Wells, Muhammad Ali, Francis Ford Coppola, Kate Meyer, and all of my friends at the Alzheimer's Foundation. Balthazar and Rosetta Getty, the Lawrence family, Jenny Lewis, Rosemary Rodriguez, Kerry Jak, Jenny Feldon, April, and John Shook for always keeping us well fed and happy. Buzz Aldrin, Michael Jackson, Bubbles, Elizabeth Taylor, John Hughes. Colee Videlle and Melissa Skoff for being with me since the beginning. Mr. Farr, Stephanie Elkin, Andy Weiss, the Robinsons, Amanda Schoun, Betsy McLaughlin, Donna and the amazing staff who take such good care of my dad, Justin Leigh and Karina, Bonnie Bruckheimer, Lucy Liu, Courtney Karp, Claire Stansfield, Ms. Sophie, Guy O' and Michelle, David Beneviste, the Sassoon family, the Mullers, Jason and Amanda,

Acknowledgments

Jason Weinberg and Merrick, Stephanie Simon and Jason Newman, Holly Robinson, Amanda de Cadenet, Mike and Stephanie Seltzer, Lisa Brenner and Dean Devlin, Janine Jones, Debbie Levin, Marsha, Thomas Butkiewicz, Duncan Bird, Casey O'Brien, and Eitan.

To all the amazing people who shared their stories and tips in this book through the "Question of the Day" or "Finish the Sentence," you added more than you'll ever know to the process and the finished product. Thank you @Vanity ace fake, Alea, Allen, Amanda, Amelia, Amy, Amy B., Amy L., AnaLiesa, AnnaMae, Annette, Ash, Ashely, Becky, Betsy, Cari, Carrie, Chaz, Collette, Dana, Danielle, Dawn, Erin, Gary, Genie, Hillary, Irene, Jan, Jason A. L., Jason G., Jeannette C., Jeannette M., Jennifer, Jessica, Jill, Jill H., Jill O.F., Joseph, JoyfulTxGal, Kathryn, Katie, Kelley K., Kelly F., Kimberly, Leslie, Lisa M., Lisa U., Luna, Marly, Mary, Mikala, Natalie, Nicole A.G., Nicole P., Paul, Retta, Sheila, Shelley. Sherill, Sherry, Stephanie, Steven, T Glass, Tazia, Tracey, Tracy, Whitney, and Yolanda.

Much love to all of the counselors at summer camp and teachers who inspired me throughout my life.

To all my animals including: Butterscotch Freeway, Georgie Porgie, Mama kitty, Hoppy, and Ellie.

About the Author

Enthusiastic, spunky, and positive, Punky Brewster was the quintessential eighties kid. Twenty-five years later, Soleil Moon Frye—the adorable girl who played her on TV—is all grown up. Today she is a married mom of two, an author, a momtrepreneur who parlayed her successful kids' clothing line into a partnership with Target, and a social media maven with over 1.4 million followers and counting.

According to Soleil, "happy chaos" is the sign of a family operating at its best—when parents accept that they'll make mistakes and will experience messes, tears, and skinned knees. Soleil currently lives in Los Angeles with her husband, Jason Goldberg, and two daughters, Poet and Jagger.